HOME DECORATING
FOR THE 90s

SMITHMARK

© 1993 Dragon's World Ltd

Photographs by Jon Bouchier, Simon Butcher, Simon Wheeler.

Illustrations by Kuo Kang Chen, Steve Cross, Paul Emra,
Pavel Kostal, Janos Marffy, Sebastian Quigley, Laurie Taylor,
Brian Watson, Andrew Green.

This edition published in 1993 by SMITHMARK Publishers Inc.,
16 East 32nd Street, New York, NY 10016.

SMITHMARK books are available for bulk purchase for sales
promotion and premium use. For details write or call the manager of
special sales, SMITHMARK Publishers Inc., 16 East 32nd Street, New
York, NY 10016; (212) 532-6600.

Produced by Dragon's World Ltd, 26 Warwick Way,
London SW1V 1RX, England.

Editor: Dorothea Hall
Designers: Bob Burroughs, Mel Raymond
Art Director: Dave Allen
Editorial Director: Pippa Rubinstein

ISBN 0-8317-4627-0

Printed in Italy

10 9 8 7 6 5 4 3 2 1

NOTICE
The authors, consultants and publishers have made
every effort to make sure the information given in this
book is reliable and accurate. They cannot accept
liability for any damage, mishap or injury arising from
the use or misuse of the information.

CONTENTS

INTRODUCTION

Your home represents a considerable investment so it makes
sense to keep it in first-class decorative condition —
both inside and out.
The following pages show the enormous variety of surface
finishes that are available for those homeowners who are
prepared to do-it-themselves. They range from the initial
preparation of the surfaces to painting, papering, staining and
wood graining, through laying carpeting and tiles to painting
the exterior of your home including the gutters and metalwork
— with plenty of professional advice and practical know-how
that will help the non-specialist home-decorator achieve lasting
results of the highest quality and lowest cost.

The purposes of decorating are two-fold: to protect interior and exterior surfaces and to bring color and character into the home. The theories about where to start and what colors to use are many but, whichever room you may choose to decorate first, there is only one place to start and that is with the preparation. Having said that, time must be given to determining color schemes and choosing which precise area to tackle first.

A lot will depend on the state of decoration of the property. On moving house, you could easily find that the exterior is in severe need of attention. Despite the fact that the rooms may also be crying out for treatment, if the weather is at all suitable – warm and dry not wet and windy – it would be unwise not to get out there straight away and add some protection before the property has to face another damaging season of high winds, rain and frost — after all, a sound exterior will protect the interior.

Coming indoors, there is little point in decorating first a room or hallway that will have to act as a thoroughfare or storage area while you decorate the rest of the house. Work out a plan of attack and finish one room completely before starting another. This really is the only way to avoid schemes that have tremendous potential but achieve nothing special because the finishing touches are missing.

Preparation

Preparing surfaces thoroughly takes time, often much more than the actual decorating. But do not create work: sound surfaces need not be stripped at all, just cleaned. Loose paint must be removed though, as must loose wallpaper, all cracks and holes filled and certain surfaces sealed. This is also the ideal time to carry out any repairs.

Exterior surfaces need cleaning and preparing in exactly the same way. The brickwork or other fabric must be sound, with cracks and holes filled, mortar renewed where necessary, woodwork re-protected against damp or infestation of woodworm, replaced if unsound, and any metalwork checked for rust and all surfaces brought up to a suitable state to accept new paintwork.

The ideal weather for exterior painting is warm and dry: late summer usually provides the right conditions. Hot sun will cause new paint to blister; if the atmosphere is damp, the paint may peel. And it is not a good idea to be working up a ladder or from a staging in a severe wind. This can obviously be avoided, and valuable time saved, by working in protected areas of the property.

Interior walls and ceilings

To prepare a room for redecoration, clear out all the furniture if at all possible. Those items that must by necessity remain should be moved to the center of the room and protected with plastic sheeting (fabric drop cloths allow paint drops to seep through). Take up the floorcovering completely or, if this is impossible, roll it back away from the walls and, again, protect with plastic sheeting. Protect varnished or polished floors with plenty of layers of paper and plastic sheeting.

Before you start any preparation, turn off the electricity supply at the mains or, if you need the light to work by, carefully protect light fittings, outlets and switches from getting wet.

New plaster

This has to be allowed to dry out completely before decoration. If the wall is to be papered eventually it needs at least 4–6 months for the moisture and salts in the plaster to come to the surface. The waiting period used to be considerably longer, with contractors recommending a full 12 months, but modern plaster dries out more efficiently and quickly. The next stage is to thoroughly prime the plaster with an alkali-resisting primer.

The only decoration that can be applied more or less immediately is latex emulsion paint; this is because it allows moisture through. Therefore, the plaster can continue its drying out process. Even then emulsion paint should not be applied until the plaster becomes lighter in color, and when it is losing its dark, wet look.

Do not sand new plaster; the surface should be beautifully smooth and sanding will only create scratches that will still be apparent when painted. Simply wipe down new plaster walls or ceilings to remove surface dust immediately before painting with latex paint.

New wallboard

The two sides of drywall sheeting are different: one side is grey, the other ivory-colored. If it has been fixed with the grey side showing it will need to be skimmed with a thin coating of finishing plaster. This must be allowed to dry before painting, as with new plaster. If the ivory side is showing and the joins between the sheets have been filled, the drywall is ready for decorating. No priming is necessary: paint or paper can be applied direct. For wall papering, hang lining paper horizontally, in the opposite direction to the wall paper, see pages 34–35.

CHAPTER 1
PREPARATION

You may be planning to redecorate your living room, paint the exterior of your house, or simply repaint the front door. Whatever the task, big or small, it is worth remembering that the finish cannot be better than the surface you have prepared. In other words, be patient with all preparatory work and do not skimp on the time involved, otherwise it will show up in the final result.

Using traditional techniques and professional advice, this chapter explains how to clean surfaces, when to strip them down, fill cracks and repair unsound areas, including reglazing a window, before attempting to apply your chosen decoration.

PREPARING WALLS

Latex-painted walls

There is no need to strip sound latex-paintwork (water based). Wash with detergent to remove all traces of grease and dirt, rinse from the top of the wall down to avoid streaks; leave to dry overnight. Scrubbing may be needed to shift heat marks near radiators, or light fittings, and to remove stains.

Particularly stubborn stains, which could show through new paintwork, can be concealed by painting the wall with aluminum primer. Household bleach will deal effectively with any signs of mildew.

Any areas of paint that are flaking or cracked should be scraped off and the surface sanded until quite smooth. Fill all holes, cracks and indentations (see opposite). Wash down to provide an absolutely sound and clean surface, prime the wall (or ceiling) with a stabilizing or multi-purpose primer before painting or papering. This stabilizes any softness in the plaster, which would otherwise become powdery and affect your final decoration. However, it may not always be necessary; the condition of the plaster will determine this.

Gloss-painted walls

Gloss (oil-based) paint is not a good decorative finish for plaster as it does not allow the surface to breathe and seals in the moisture. It used to be popular in kitchens and bathrooms where it was seen as a foil against condensation and could be washed down easily but, with today's washable latex paint finishes, there is no benefit in using gloss.

If you are faced with such a wall, do not attempt to strip the paint; it would take forever. (Blowtorches and hot air strippers, which speed the process of stripping gloss, are not suitable for use on plastered surfaces.)

Wash the wall thoroughly with water and detergent to rid it of grease and dirt, rinse, allow to dry then deal with any damaged areas. Scrape off flaking paint, using a flat scraper or shave hook, and sand until perfectly smooth. Fill cracks, holes and indentations (see above) then sand the entire wall to provide a "key" for new paintwork. Prime any bare plaster.

Whitewashed surfaces

The whole area must be stripped as this finish is very unstable and new paint or paper will not adhere properly. Water and detergent used with a stiff-bristled banister brush and sponge will be effective if the paint has been applied direct to plaster. If it is

Sanding an enamel-painted wall to provide a key for new paintwork; use medium sandpaper around a cork block or a foam-filled abrasive pad.

Removing whitewash with a stiff bristle scrubbing brush, water and detergent before applying a stabilising primer.

backed with lining paper, then the paper will have to be stripped with it. Soapy water or wallpaper remover left to soak in will help to soften the paper sufficiently for it to be removed with a flat scraper. The surface should then be thoroughly cleaned to remove all traces of the original coating and effectively sealed with a coat of stabilizing primer, a multi-purpose primer to ensure stability, and to provide a sound surface ready for the next stage of either hanging wallpaper or painting.

Papered surfaces

If the wallpaper is perfectly sound and stuck firmly to the surface it will probably not need stripping. However, it is not a good idea to build up too many layers though, and stripping could prove advisable for this reason alone. If several layers are allowed to build up, it will become impossibly difficult to remove them without specialist equipment and a good deal of time. Another instance when sound paper may need to be stripped is if the dyes in the pattern are not fast and the surface is to be painted rather than papered. This is easily tested: dab some paint onto the paper and if the colors show any sign of running, either strip the paper completely or apply a good covering of aluminum primer to seal it. Another alternative, if there are not too many layers of paper already, would be to cover the existing patterned paper with plain lining paper (see page 35). Small damaged areas of paper can be sanded smooth and lifting corners or torn pieces can be restuck with paste to give a firm, smooth surface.

To clean wallpaper: brush down with a soft-bristled brush. The room must be left for at least 24 hours to allow dust to settle. (It is preferable to use a vacuum cleaner attachment for this job as it cuts down on dust considerably.)

Stripping wallpaper from plaster

Unless the covering is vinyl, which just peels away from its paper backing, soaking and scraping are the techniques used here: the important thing is to leave the paper to soak thoroughly. Warm water works just as well by itself as when it is mixed with wallpaper stripper if it is allowed to penetrate and soften the paste on the wall.

To aid penetration, especially when the paper has been painted over or is heavily embossed, scratch the wallpaper with a wire brush or coarse glasspaper to allow the liquid through more easily. Sponge or spray on the water from a houseplant sprayer.

Work from top to bottom, doing one width of paper at a time. Use the scraper carefully, holding it at an angle that will lift the paper but not damage the plaster underneath. Special wallpaper scrapers are available in different widths and weights, which allow you to strip off old wallpaper easily without danger of scoring the wall surface.

When the wall is bare, scrub off any remaining paste and sponge the surface clean ready for filling and making good.

Steam strippers can be rented to facilitate stripping very thick paper or layer upon layer. They are not that much quicker and are tiring to use, as a metal sole plate from which the steam emerges has to be held against the wall until the paste and paper have softened. Again, scratching the paper in advance speeds the process.

Stripping wallpaper from wallboard

It is not advisable to strip paper from drywall, even if it has been primed beneath the paper, as the water could soak through and ruin the drywall itself, or the scraper cause irreparable damage. Restick any areas that may be lifting, sand smooth areas that are scratched or torn and coat with aluminum primer if the colors in the pattern show signs of running, or cross-hang with lining paper to cover all imperfections (see page 35).

Exterior walls

Many people choose to paint only the trim outside their house, leaving the walls in their natural state. Once painted, brickwork, stone, stucco or any other fabric will have to be maintained that way on a regular basis; to strip the paint completely would be an unthinkable task. The preparation for painting will depend on the existing condition. Start at the top of the wall.

Unpainted brickwork/rendering/stone

Scrub down with plain water but if there are signs of efflorescence (a white residue), which is the natural salts in the bricks, brush off with a stiff *dry* brush. Water will aggravate the problem. Do not use a wire brush as it will leave marks and if bits of wire break loose they will rust and spoil the finish.

Carry out any repairs that are needed (see below), then, if leaving unpainted, brush on a colorless water-repellent treatment. This will prevent rain penetrating the fabric of the walls without affecting their natural appearance.

If the wall is to be painted, first prime with a stabilizing primer but only if the surface is powdery, alkaline or stained. Paint within days of priming for the most successful results.

Painted brickwork/rendering/stone

If the surface is sound just give it a thorough brushing down with a banister brush; if dirty, scrub with detergent, rinse and leave to dry. Scrape away any loose or flaking paint. Deal with any repairs (see below) and apply a coat of stabilizing primer if the surface is at all powdery. If the wall is painted with a cement-based paint, which is unwashable, brush and scrape it clean. Having dealt with repairs, apply a stabilizing primer to give a solid surface on which to re-decorate.

Common faults

Algae To remedy the problem which is caused by

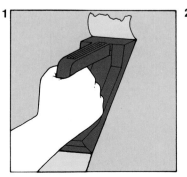

1 Removing wallpaper with a stripper; a roller in the base ensures that the blade does not dig into the plaster.
2 Using a steam-stripper for stubborn paper; hold the sole plate against the wall and strip off the paper when saturated with steam.
3 Removing efflorescence; use a stiff bristle brush without water as the salts will dissolve and the problem will recur.

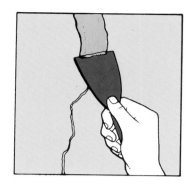

Filling cracks in plaster; undercut the edges to provide a key for the filler, brush out debris and fill with a filling knife.

Repairing damaged rough stucco; after renewing the mortar, throw on the aggregate while it is still wet and press in with a wooden float.

damp, apply a fungicide solution, following the manufacturer's instructions. Hose off the solution using a hand-brush attachment.

Moss/mold Apply diluted bleach (1 part bleach: 4 parts water) and scrape off growth when dry. Apply bleach again and leave to dry. A fungicide solution can also be used.

Water stains Caused by defective guttering/down pipes or dripping windowsills. Having remedied the defect, allow the stain to dry then apply an alkali-resistant primer to stop the stain coming through.

Cracks in surface or gaps by doors/windows Fill with an exterior filler.

Broken/cracked bricks For these larger areas, use a cement mortar as a filler. Rake out loose material. Undercut the edges of wider cracks and holes using a sledge hammer and cold chisel and brush away dust. Paint with a PVA bonding agent and press in the mortar. If the hole is deep, do this in two stages, scratching the first layer to give a grip for the second and leaving it to dry completely. Smooth off the top layer with a builder's trowel or float.

Missing rough stucco Remove any loose material and hack back to bare bricks, undercutting the edges of the hole. Apply a PVA bonding agent to the hole. Spread on cement mortar. While still wet, throw suitably sized aggregate onto the surface to the same density as the original stucco, press in with a wood float and leave to set. If the wall is to be painted the color of the aggregate is immaterial.

Repointing brickwork The mortar between bricks will inevitably need renewal in some areas. Chisel out the mortar from the vertical then the horizontal joints. Brush away dust. Trowel mortar into the joints; uprights first. Apply a pointing profile to match the surrounding wall.

Repairing interior walls

When working outside, exterior grade filler must be used; inside, however, interior or exterior fillers are suitable. You can buy powder fillers for mixing with water, which is most economical, or ready-mixed types in tubs for convenient use.

Cracks Using the edge of a flat scraper, rake out any loose material. Mix the filler according to the manufacturer's instructions (or scoop straight from the tub) and press into the crack with the scraper. Overfill slightly, as most fillers tend to shrink and will leave indentations. Smooth off with a wet blade and leave to dry. When hard, sand level with surrounding surface, using medium-grade and then fine-grade glasspaper.

Indentations Slight fluctuations in the surface will ruin the effect when exposed under lighting and should be brought up level using a fine-surface filler. Simply press in the filler, leave to dry and sand down to a glossy smooth finish.

Holes Small holes should be dealt with like cracks. Large holes should be filled with finishing plaster rather than filler. Having removed all loose material and undercut the edges with a cold chisel, wet the hole and then press in the plaster with a trowel. Do this in two stages if it is easier, scoring a criss-cross pattern on the plaster and allowing it to dry before adding a second layer. Filler can be used on top to bring it up to the general level of the surface. Sand smooth. With a really deep and wide hole some backing material may be necessary to support the filling substance. Crumpled chicken wire or dampened, screwed-up newspaper can both be used.

Corners Temporarily fix a wood batten to one edge of the corner with two nails. Dampen and fill in the other edge by scraping filler against the batten. When dry, release the batten, sand smooth the filled edge and nail the batten over. Fill in the second edge.

Uneven surface If the untreatable irregularities spread all over the wall, hang a thickly embossed lining paper or use a textured paint (see page 28).

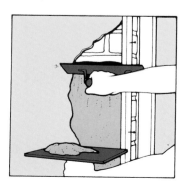

Repairing a damaged corner after fixing a temporary guide batten to one face; when the plaster is dry, repeat for the other face.

PREPARING WOODWORK

The techniques for preparing wood to give a firm surface for the new coats of paint are the same both inside and outside the house. Stripping wood takes a long time and, as it is unnecessary to strip sound surfaces, strip only the faulty areas. There will be times when complete stripping is unavoidable: for example, to bring a built-in cabinet back to its natural finish when it is to remain unpainted. Several layers of paint are, in fact, an effective protector for the wood, so never strip it simply for this reason, although it could be preferable if the molded detail has been lost beneath the layers.

Once the damaged areas have been stripped, dust down and prime bare wood. Fill in any defects, prime the filling and sand down the whole surface to provide a key for painting. Always follow the grain of the wood when sanding to avoid scratching. The smoothest finish is achieved with the wet-and-dry abrasive paper used wet. If working by hand, fasten a length of glasspaper (cut to fit the exact width) around a block of wood, measuring approximately 4in × 5in × 1in deep. This will greatly facilitate sanding large flat areas, such as door panels and inside the recesses. When the glasspaper becomes clogged up or worn, unfasten it and move it around the block to give a fresh area of glasspaper. A powered orbital sander will greatly speed up the sanding of large flat areas that need keying.

Stripping interior woodwork

The main areas are: doors, windows, baseboards, stairs and banisters and decorative features such as architraves, picture rails, built-in cabinets, dado rails and wainscotting. There are three ways recommended to strip paint or varnish from woodwork: dry scraping, heat stripping and chemical stripping.

Dry scraping Suitable for small areas only. Scrape the flaking paint off with a hook scraper or a shavehook (the combination shavehook, having a straight and a curved edge, is particularly good on moldings). Sand the small bare patches level with medium- then fine-grade glasspaper.

Heat stripping The one recommended way to apply heat to paint is with an electric hot-air gun. This is a fairly recent innovation preferable for several reasons to the old-fashioned blowtorch, which is now considered dangerous. With a hot-air gun there is no flame, and there is far less likelihood of scorching the wood, which is important if you want to leave the surface bare.

Using a hot air gun

Allow the stripper to heat up before starting. Holding it about 1 inch from the surface, wave it over the area of woodwork to be stripped. Watch for the softening of the paint – which will very quickly blister and bubble – then draw a shavehook firmly down, removing the layers of paint and undercoat in one complete operation. Move the stripper just ahead of the shavehook and always use this in a downward motion.

The oil-based paint hardens quickly on cooling, so it is better to try to scrape it off immediately. Catch the hot paint droppings on layers of newspaper, ready to be bundled up for disposal. A flat scraper can be used successfully on flat expanses of wood, with an upward movement, but the shavehook is best as its shape prevents any gouging of the wood. Any serious gouging would, of course, need filling with an appropriate wood filler before moving on to the next stage in the preparation.

You will find that most undercoats will lift off with the top coat but any residue, or any slight scorching that will occur with a stripper that is handled without care, can be sanded down when the stripping is complete.

To avoid scorching the wood, never hold the hot air stripper over one area continuously. After all, the paint needs only to melt in order for the shavehook to scrape it away. It is better to deal with moldings first, as they are the most intricate parts, and remember always to shield adjacent areas from the heat. This obviously applies particularly to the glass in windows and doors. A piece of board firmly secured in place will suffice.

Most hot air guns come with a selection of optional nozzles for concentrating the jet of hot air. You will find that a wide, narrow mouth is ideal for use on thin glazing bars and other finely molded areas such as fireplace surrounds. You will find it better to experiment beforehand on a spare piece of painted wood.

Stripping paint from a windowsill with a hot air gun; direct it ahead of a shave hook and scrape the paint as soon as it blisters.

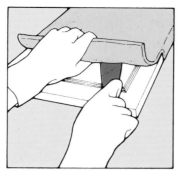

Using paint-stripper around a window; brush on and follow with a scraper as soon as the paint surface blisters.

Stripping paint from moldings with a paste stripper; apply with a trowel, leave as recommended and peel off with the paint.

Chemical stripping

There are two ways to strip paint chemically; with liquid or with paste. The liquid is best for windows as there is no danger of damaging the glass. Wear protective rubber gloves and follow the instructions on the container carefully.

Dab the stripper on, leave for 15–20 minutes and scrape off the blistering paint. Be particularly careful where the shavings fall and protect any floor-covering efficiently using drop sheets and newspaper. This can be wrapped and the shavings disposed of. Wash down the stripped wood with water or white spirit (according to the maker's instructions) and leave to dry overnight. Smooth all over with medium-grade glass-paper.

Chemical paste is particularly useful on moldings (which are fiddly to strip by any other method) and for overhead use, where liquid would drip. Trowel the paste on and leave to do its work. Test its efficacy at intervals and lift off in a complete "sheet" when it has worked through all the layers of paint. Scrub clean and leave to dry overnight.

Chemical stripping is best for areas that are to retain their natural wood finish as there is no danger of scorching.

Priming the wood

The priming of bare wood should be done before any filling is carried out. Acrylic or multi-purpose primers are both acceptable for interior woodwork. Shellac-based wood primer should be used where stains or preservatives could cause discoloration in the final decorative finish. Shellac-based primer is also used on oily or resinous woods such as teak and cedar, for the same reason.

A second application of primer is needed on damaged areas once any defects have been filled and knots treated.

Filling defects

For interior woodwork a plaster filler is acceptable but if the filling is in an area that is likely to be affected by the weather (window frame) or damp, exterior-grade filler or one of the many proprietary brands specially devised for woodwork would be better.

The damaged area having been stripped and primed, press the filling agent into the hole and smooth over with a filling knife. Leave to dry then sand smooth. Prime the filled area.

Knotting

Knots are immediately obvious on new wood, and if left untreated they will ooze resin and cause any paint covering to discolor or lift.

Strip any coating away. Applying heat to the knots will draw out the resin, which can be wiped away with white spirit.

Apply two coats of shellac knotting with a small brush or cloth before priming: to stop any remaining resin from seeping out and discoloring the decoration.

Applying shellac knotting to a knot in bare wood to prevent the resin from oozing out and staining the paintwork when applied.

Stripping other finishes

As an alternative finish, interior woodwork may have been varnished, oiled or waxed.

Varnish is stripped in exactly the same way as for paint, with heat or a chemical stripper greatly speeding the process.

Oil or wax is best removed with white spirit and steel wool, following the grain of the wood. Wipe clean with absorbent paper and repeat the process until all signs of the coating are gone. Paint will not adhere to oil or wax. Scrub thoroughly with detergent and dry before priming. Any discoloration in the wood can be remedied with wood-color restorer.

Exterior woodwork

Wash sound surfaces with a sugar soap solution. To achieve a good key for fresh paint, rub down while still wet with wet-and-dry abrasive paper, used dry.

Rinse down to remove dust, and leave to dry overnight.

Any flaking, peeling, chipped or split paint must be removed back to the bare wood. The methods of stripping are as for interior woodwork. The hot air stripper or blowlamp will be the quickest and most efficient on large areas. Reserve the chemical stripper for windows or where a natural finish is wanted.

Eavesboards, fascias and soffits

As all the woodwork of eavesboards, fascias and soffits is above eye level the principal purpose is protection rather than appearance. Clear away all debris and scrape clean. Use a flat scraper and hot air

•CHECKPOINT•

Decayed wood

While stripping the exterior paint keep an eye open for irregularities in the surface. Although the paint coat may look sound, the wood beneath could be soft and crumbling. Probe gently with a knife. If the wood is soft it will need repair or replacement. For lesser damage, hack out the soft wood and use a wood repair system.

One available system is used in three stages: firstly, a chemical wood hardener is painted on to give a sound, firm base. A high performance wood filler is used next to make the repair, which will expand and contract with the wood and special pellets of preservative are then fitted into pre-drilled holes surrounding the repair. These act on the basis that once the moisture content in the wood rises to a level when rot can start, the pellets dissolve and release preservative before any damage can be done.

Applying high-performance wood filler to a rotten windowsill after treating with hardener; finally insert pellets.

stripper with an extension cord, or a blowtorch, to remove flaking paint (being particularly careful near the eaves as fire is a genuine hazard). If this can be avoided, simply sand the entire surface of the board and prime any areas that need filling. Use an exterior grade filler or waterproof stopping and smooth it with a filling knife. When dry, prime the entire surface.

Wall siding

This will be the single largest area of exterior woodwork on any house. If it is new and is to be left with its natural finish, it must be coated with a water-repellent wood preservative for protection against damp. Colored preservative can also be bought as an alternative.

If the wood is varnished or painted, sand down following the grain. Prime and fill holes and other defects before priming the entire surface ready for redecorating. If you are painting new wood siding that has been treated with a preservative coating, use an aluminum wood primer to prevent any discoloration to the final decoration.

PREPARING METALWORK

The prime purpose of decorating metalwork is to protect it against tarnish and corrosion, especially outside the home. Ferrous metals (iron and steel) are particularly prone to rusting. Both new and tarnished metal surfaces must be carefully prepared before painting. Rust is a particular problem which can be dealt with in several ways.

Heat strippers are ineffective on metal; the metal absorbs the heat and the paint does not soften but instead becomes baked on. Use a wire brush to scrape off the flaky paint and rust and if necessary, a chemical stripper.

Priming of bare metal is essential, as primers contain a rust-inhibitor which protects the metal against further corrosion.

Cast iron steel

For new metal, clean thoroughly with white spirit used with emery paper to remove grease. Remove any rust particles with a wire brush. Apply a zinc chromate primer.

For tarnished metal, scrape down thoroughly with a wire brush to remove all loose paint and rust, right back to "bright" metal (this does not mean that the metal must shine, however). An electric drill wire cup brush attachment will speed this process (see facing page). Dust off and treat with zinc chromate primer.

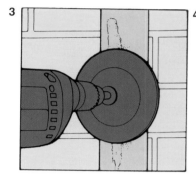

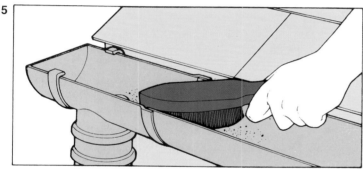

1 Rubbing off loose rust with steel wool before treating the area with rust remover; follow manufacturer's guide for surface preparation.
2 Coating the surface with metal primer immediately after treatment; with some rust removers, the enamel paint can be applied direct.
3 Removing flaking rust with an abrasive disc and an electric drill; a flap sanding attachment works equally well.

4 Using a wire brush attachment in an electric drill to remove rust from intricate shapes; a cup-shaped brush is also available.
5 After removing debris with a masonite scraper cut to the shape of the guttering, rubbing down rust with a wire brush.

Small items such as door knobs, letterplates and other decorative pieces are easily stripped of paint by immersion in a solution of caustic soda (tie lengths of wire to them for retrieval). Use a plastic bucket and wear protective rubber gloves and goggles. When stripped clean, rinse well and dry quickly or rusting will occur.

Galvanized metal

This is coated with zinc to protect against rust but the galvanizing can chip or wear off, exposing the steel. When cleaning take care not to remove or damage this coating.

For new metal, clean thoroughly to remove grease with a rag dipped in white spirit. Treat with a calcium plumbate primer.

For tarnished metal, a chemical stripper would harm the zinc coating, so brush down with a wire brush to remove loose paint. Brush lightly, taking care not to scratch the surface. Remove grease with white spirit and treat with zinc chromate primer.

Aluminum and other non-ferrous metal

For new metal, aluminum (windows, for example) need not be decorated. If it is to be, rub down with fine emery paper, clean with white spirit applied with a rag and treat with a zinc chromate primer.

For tarnished metal, scrape or brush away any signs of corrosion, being careful not to scratch the metal surface. Dust off and prime with a zinc chromate primer.

Indoor metalwork

Central heating pipes are usually concealed beneath the floorboards and it is only where solid floors intervene that the pipework is commonly surface-mounted. It can be left as it is or painted to match the decoration on the supporting wall.

A thorough rub down with abrasive paper will remove any loose surface material and any corrosion that may have appeared where water has dripped onto the pipes (when bleeding radiators, for example). Drips will collect underneath pipes so always check there for rust. Any bare areas should be primed with a zinc chromate primer prior to painting.

Radiators should be treated in the same way. All signs of rust should be removed. New radiators (and

Using abrasive paper wrapped around a sponge to rub down curved areas; a flexible sanding block is a useful alternative.

window frames) are supplied ready-primed but, where this has been chipped and the primer removed, clean the area and prime again otherwise the new paint will not adhere well.

Windows should be scraped and rubbed down to remove all rust. Check the condition of the putty and, if necessary, renew (see glazing a window, page 17). Prime any bare metal with a rust-inhibiting primer prior to painting.

Exterior metalwork

Gates and railings Undoubtedly, the most common problem here is rust. The moldings and lack of flat surfaces will make stripping painfully slow, so the simplest course of action is to remove paint and loose rust from the affected areas either mechanically or with a wire brush, then treat as shown in the Checkpoint box below.

Gutters

Blockages Clear all leaves and debris from gutters before attempting any other preparation. Clear out hopper heads and replace mesh guards in the tops of downpipes securing them firmly.

Cracks Having cleaned the pipe or length of guttering and removed all rust, fill the cracks with a waterproof caulk.

Leaking joints These will be instantly obvious as they will have caused corrosion of the surrounding area. Lengths of guttering are joined by being overlapped, the joint sealed with caulk and then securely bolted. To repair a leaking joint, the bolts can be released and the caulk seal renewed. Alternatively, you can make a temporary seal by applying caulk to the join on the inside of the gutter without releasing the bolts. Similarly, seal leaking joints in downpipes with caulking in the same way.

•CHECKPOINT•

Removing/neutralizing paint

There are several proprietary products available for removing flaking paint from metal-work and dealing with rust.

Rust removing
When using a rust remover, the uppermost, loose layer is best removed mechanically with a wire brush attachment to an electric drill. These come in various shapes: a cup brush of 2 to 3in diameter will cope in most situations. A hand-held wire brush can be used on small areas.

Daub the rust remover liberally onto the rusted areas only, not the entire surface and leave for about 15 minutes. Apply a second thin coat of remover and wipe dry with a clean cloth. In about another 30 minutes the patches will be ready for a coat of primer and this should be applied to the entire surface to protect the metal against further corrosion.

Chemical neutralizing agents
As well as rust removers there are chemical rust neutralizing agents, which actually act on the rust itself, converting it into an inert metallic coat ready for redecoration. There is no need to brush away the loose rust. Apply a thick coat of the agent all over the rusted area. Leave it to harden slightly for about an hour and then wipe away any excess from the surrounding areas with mineral spirit applied with a rag.

After 24 hours wash the area with water and leave to dry. No priming is necessary before painting but, if the entire metal surface is to be redecorated, the rest of the metal will need to be primed with a rust-inhibiting primer.

Special rust neutralizers are available for use on chrome, where no paint is to be applied.

After treating ironwork with rust remover, wash off well and prime with a general purpose primer.

This rust converter requires no priming; it changes the rust into an inert compound which can be painted directly.

Ideal for central-heating radiators, this treatment dries to a smooth flat white finish suitable for repainting.

Reglazing a window

When you are redecorating windows it is likely that you will have to repair defective, crumbly putty seals and even replace panes of glass that have been cracked.

The normal thickness of glass for a window is $\frac{1}{8}$in. When ordering the new pane, measure $\frac{1}{8}$in less each way than the space inside the rebate to allow for fitting tolerance. It is unlikely that a wood frame will be exactly square, so as well as measuring all four sides, measure the diagonals before buying the glass. Buying the right sized glass will save a lot of time as trimming is not easy.

If there is beading on top of the putty remove this first by prising it away from the center. Stick strips of adhesive tape across the broken pane in criss-cross fashion then, wearing thick gloves, tap out the fragments, letting the glass fall carefully onto many layers of newspaper, which can be parceled up for safe disposal.

Hack out the old putty with an old wood chisel or a glazier's hacking knife, taking care not to gouge the frame. Pull out the glazing tacks and set aside for re-use. Clean down the exposed rebate, scraping away any flaking paint, and prime it.

Use linseed oil putty for a wood frame (or an all-purpose type). Knead the putty until it is pliable. Roll the putty into long sausage-shapes and press into the rebate with your thumb.

Lift the glass into place, pressing it into the putty at the bottom, around the edges, then at the top. Do not press the center of the pane or it may crack. Replace the tacks (or use panel pins), knocking them into the frame with the cross pein of a pin hammer (or use the back of a putty knife). If the hammer head or knife is slid against the pane all the time the glass is far less likely to be broken accidentally. Press another sausage of putty all round the glass, then smooth to a neat bevel with a putty knife; trim off excess both inside and out. Make a mitered joint at each corner then run a paintbrush over the smoothed putty to make sure it adheres to the glass and has formed a watertight seal. Leave the putty to harden for 48 hours before cleaning the glass with methylated spirit. Paint the putty after two weeks.

For metal windows use special metal casement putty. Glazings clips are used in place of sprigs and, again, can be re-used. Note their position in the frame for replacement. Scrape away any rust to base metal and treat the frame with a rust-inhibiting sealer. Secure the new pane with putty and glazing clips.

Removing broken window glass; criss-cross with masking tape to prevent pieces from falling out, and wear gloves.

After removing all fragments of glass, chiseling out the old putty; pull out glazing tacks with pliers and retain.

Applying a bead putty to the rebate in the frame after first coating it with a suitable primer.

After pressing in the glass around the edges, tapping in the tacks; slide the hammer across the glass.

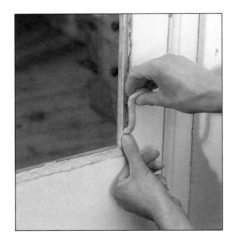

With the glass secured in the rebate, applying a covering bead of putty to seal it in.

Mitering the corners after smoothing with a putty knife; finally brush over with a clean paintbrush.

CHAPTER 2

PAINTING THE HOME

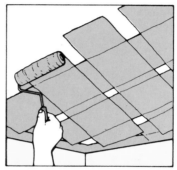

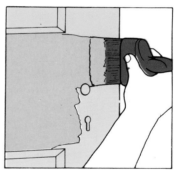

There is always a certain build-up of excitement as decorating gets underway — and the newly finished surfaces give character and style to your chosen scheme.
The following pages give details of the correct types of paint to use on specific surfaces, how to apply paint correctly to walls and woodwork — focusing special attention on windows and doors. This is followed by an extensive selection of traditional paint finishes, from rag rolling and stenciling to applying textured paint and graining wood. Supported by professionally written how-to instructions, these excellent finishes will give you pride and pleasure in your home for many years to come.

PAINTING WALLS

The equipment needed for painting in the home is fairly minimal and the initial outlay will serve as an investment in that most items can be used, cleaned and stored ready for re-use.

Equipment

Brushes in several sizes are needed, the ideal width for painting large areas being 4 to 6in. Narrower 1 and 2in brushes will be needed for woodwork. Two useful extras are a cutting-in brush, with bristles angled to cut in on narrow window glazing bars, for example, and a radiator brush, for painting behind radiators and pipes and in awkward corners.

Clean brushes immediately after use – in water for latex paint and with mineral spirit for gloss. A brush can be stored overnight without cleaning by being suspended in water or white spirit; the bristles must not touch the bottom of the container. Shake and wipe dry before use the following day.

Rollers come in different sizes and fabrics including one for painting behind radiators. They are often interchangeable. They are quicker on large areas than brushes, often giving a better finish, but use more paint and tend to spatter. Foam-covered rollers are the cheapest; they are also the worst spatterers. Cleaning is more difficult than with brushes and cleaning oil-based paint from a foam roller is probably not worth the trouble.

Paint pads comprising a pile stuck to a foam back, do not spatter and give a good smooth finish. Various sizes are available, plus extension handles and replacement heads. Pads are good on textured papers and woven surfaces.

A paint kettle is useful when doing a lot of painting. An old paint can with a handle will do; fix a strip of wire across it against which the brush can be wiped.

Ladders comprising two step-ladders with a staging plank between is the ideal arrangement when painting up high, as it avoids having to go up and down the ladder all the time. A stool is also very useful. Remember that such equipment can be rented.

Using and storing paint

Coverage is given in square feet and varies between manufacturers. To find the quantity needed, multiply the height of the room by the perimeter measurement. Make deductions for large doors and windows.

Stir all liquid paints well before use. Turning the can upside down for some hours will help redistribute the paint particles.

• CHECKPOINT •

Types of paint for indoor use

Latex paint
Latex paint comprises particles of synthetic resin – acrylic or vinyl – mixed with pigment (which gives the paint its color) suspended in water. When the water evaporates a film forms on the surface, which is permeable, allowing moisture to pass through.

Quick-drying, latex is also easy to apply to interior walls and ceilings and a number of materials – plaster, gypsumboard, wood, synthetic boards, brick and cement render, and brushes and equipment are easily cleaned. Two finishes are available: flat and satin (semi-gloss) both of which are tough, hardwearing and easy to clean (especially the latter). The flat finish is better on surfaces that have been filled and repaired, as the non-shiny finish helps to conceal irregularities.

Non-drip thixotropic latex combines good one-coat coverage, excellent spreadability and largely splash-free application.

Solid latex in white and tinted tones offers non-drip, non-spatter application by roller or brush, making it ideal for use on ceilings or where you cannot remove a floorcovering but do not trust your ability to avoid splashes and drips.

Latex paints can be thinned with water as a priming coat for porous surfaces, such as new plaster.

Gloss enamel paint
Solvent-based (oil) paints comprise pigment, binder (which makes it stick to the surface you are painting and resists damp), and a drier to speed up the rate at which the paint dries. These ingredients are suspended in a solvent or "thinner" such as mineral spirit. A compatible oil-based undercoat is needed as a flat, obliterating matt base for the shiny top coat (which dries to give a water-resistant finish that is durable enough to withstand day-to-day knocks). Enamel paint is commonly used for woodwork and is not really suitable for decorating walls. Non-drip thixotropic enamel needs no undercoat and, applied thickly, gives better coverage; only one coat may be needed. It avoids the problems of runs and drips that can occur with liquid enamel. There is a wide selection of colors and tints to choose from.

Eggshell/semi gloss
If a gloss-type finish is required on walls, this resin-based paint is the one to choose. It is steam resistant, like enamel and therefore particularly suited to use in kitchens and bathrooms. It can be used on both walls, ceilings and woodwork.

Textured paint
Extremely efficient in masking general unevenness in a wall or ceiling surface, or a mass of hairline cracks, textured paint comes in two types: ready-mixed and powder form. The former needs no over-painting and is available in a range of colors.

The powder form has to be mixed with water and comes in white only; it is designed to be painted over. Both types can be applied using a short pile or foam roller or paintbrush for a random effect, or you can impress it with a variety of interesting patterns (see page 28).

APPLYING PAINT

It is important to work in good light, preferably natural, to ensure even coverage of the paint. If you have to work in artificial light, remove the shade and use a high-wattage bulb.

In all rooms, paint the ceiling first. If using two stepladders and a scaffold board, set these up across the window wall. With a single ladder, set this up at one end of the window wall.

Using a brush

Apply the paint with a wide 4 to 6in brush: dip only the first third of the bristles into the paint and wipe off excess on the edge of the kettle. Work across the ceiling, back from the window, in strips 2ft wide. Turn the brush on its edge to paint a band round the edge of the ceiling, working right into the wall. The overlap will either be covered by paint on the wall or by wallpaper. Then turn the brush full face and proceed to paint in strips. When you are applying latex, you are not governed by a strict painting pattern, as it does not readily form solid lines.

Using a roller

A paint roller will speed the operation considerably, which is always welcome, as painting a ceiling can be tiring for the arms and neck.

Paint a band around the room using a brush: the roller cannot reach into the ceiling/wall angle. To avoid spatters, load the roller with paint and remove the excess by rolling it on the ribbed end of the tray, out of the paint. Keep the roller close to the surface all the time and apply the paint in criss-cross strokes, picking up the wet edges of adjoining star shapes formed to coat the whole area. "Lay off" by rolling in one direction only, parallel to one wall, and using very light strokes.

After cutting in around the edges of a ceiling, covering the area with diagonal strokes in alternate directions.

Finishing the ceiling by working towards the window with straight strokes of the roller parallel to the side wall.

1 After cutting in at the wall/ceiling angle with a small brush, brushing in horizontal bands working from the top downwards.
2 Covering the horizontal strokes at the top of the wall with vertical strokes, before the paint dries, to ensure good coverage.

3 After cutting in at corners with a small brush, applying paint with a roller; start at a corner, with the handle away from the side wall.
4 Overlapping with criss-cross strips; paint 10sq ft at a time and make angled strokes off the edges to start the next patch.

Use a brush on any moldings, and use a brush to apply paint around them.

Walls

If you are using two ladders and a staging board, work in bands across the room, from the top of the wall to the bottom. If using only one ladder, work in strips down each wall. Keep the strips about 18in wide in order not to lean out dangerously from the ladder. Do not keep the edges of the strips straight or they will be more difficult to blend.

Never leave painting a wall incomplete: the paint will dry and it will be obvious where it was taken up again by a hard ridge. If you are using more than one can of paint, stir the second can thoroughly and mix some of it in the paint kettle with the remains of the first can. There should not be an obvious variation in color but any minor difference will be minimized.

Semi gloss enamel paint needs more careful application than latex. Paint it on in downward strokes and lay off in light horizontal strokes, without reloading the brush with paint. Always lay off from

Using a compressed-gas-powered paint roller; thinned paint in the canister is fed to the roller by a carbon dioxide capsule in the lid.

Making horizontal sweeps with an electric sprayer before following up with vertical sweeps; adjust for even coverage without splutter.

one strip to the next carefully to ensure even coverage.

As with painting ceilings, a roller is speedy on walls, except where textured paint has been used previously. When using a brush on such surfaces, it will be necessary to use a stippling movement to paint into the deep indentations.

Spray painting

For exceptional swiftness when painting walls, you will find a spray gun supreme. Guns that can be bought or rented, are either electrically-powered or worked by pump action and can be used with latex or gloss paints.

What slows the spraying down is the need to mask off anything not to be painted. This is why it is only worth considering spraying on large areas: you will have to mask off the baseboards and floor, taping the sheets down with masking tape. The same must be done with switches, outlets and light fixtures. Newspaper spread around the floor close to the walls (over the polythene) will soak up any flying spray. This cannot be stressed too much. It is better to spend time on masking all surfaces not to be painted than running the risk of causing serious accidents.

Apply the paint in horizontal bands but spray the two sides of an interior corner separately; moldings and external corners should be given an initial coat then painted again with the whole wall for sufficient depth of color. For an even coverage, keep the nozzle at right angles to the wall, 6 to 8in away, and do not swing it from side to side.

PAINTING INSIDE WOODWORK

Having followed the instructions for the preparation of woodwork (see page 12), the surface should be sound, smooth, primed and under-coated ready for painting. Special undercoats may be recommended with certain gloss colors, so check the paint chart or the can. One coat of primer and one of undercoat is normally followed by two coats of gloss.

Doors

The entire door must be painted in one session. Wipe down to remove dust immediately beforehand and arrange newspaper on the floor to catch any drips.

Paneled doors. There is a sequence that must be followed when painting paneled doors, affected slightly by whether it opens towards or away from the painter. Opening towards the painter, the top edge and opening edge should be painted first; away from the painter, the hinged edge is painted first. From then on, the sequence is the same.

Paint the moldings and the panels in the top of the door then those at the bottom. Follow these with the central vertical section and the three horizontal cross sections (top, middle, bottom). Finally, paint the two outer vertical sections working downwards from the top. When the door itself has been finished, move on to the frame and casing.

Flush doors. Quick confident painting is the answer. Divide the door mentally into four. Paint the top two

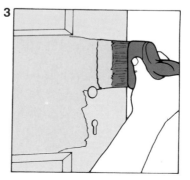

1 Applying enamel paint along the grain of a paneled door; blend together adjacent strokes as you proceed across the door.
2 After completing the horizontal strokes, painting across the grain with a loaded brush to ensure full and even coverage.
3 Painting towards the edge of the door to prevent paint from being scraped onto the edge and forming a corner ridge.

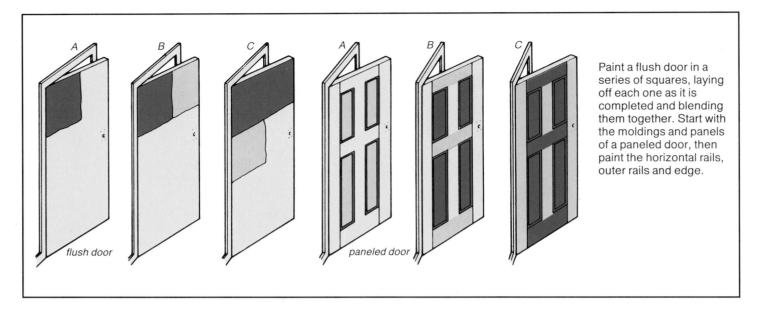

Paint a flush door in a series of squares, laying off each one as it is completed and blending them together. Start with the moldings and panels of a paneled door, then paint the horizontal rails, outer rails and edge.

flush door

paneled door

sections first, then the bottom two. Speed is essential to avoid a hard edge forming between the sections as the paint dries. The correct application of paint to large flat areas like the flush doors is particularly important (see below).

Glazed doors. The glass should be protected from the paint. Either stick masking tape around the edge or use lengths of double-sided tape with newspaper stuck on top to cover all the glass. Do not leave either tape too long or it will be difficult to remove, especially if the sun has been shining onto the glass from behind. Also in removing the tape when the paint has hardened, paint may pull away with it leaving a ragged edge.

Using oil-based gloss paint

In painting with gloss paint, there is a sequence of laying on, cross-brushing, smoothing out and laying off which should be followed. First of all, using a length of wood, stir the paint to blend in the solvent.

The brush should not be heavily loaded. Holding the brush in a pencil grip – fingers on the ferrule (metal band), thumb hooked behind the stem – dip about one-third of the length of the bristles into the paint. Press the brush against the wire over the paint can to remove the excess. Lay on the paint with vertical strokes.

Without reloading the brush, cross-brush the adjoining section. Smooth the two sections together, again with horizontal strokes and without reloading the brush. Lay off with light vertical strokes, drawing the brush upwards away from the wet edge.

Move down the door and follow the same sequence, laying off the paint into the top section. With

wood, lay off the paint in the direction of the grain.

Sags and runs are caused by an overloaded brush or the paint being applied unevenly and not cross-brushed. When the first coat is completely dry, rub down any faults with fine glasspaper. A second and, possibly, a third coat of gloss will cover these areas completely. To ensure a really smooth finish and good adhesion between coats of paint, give a light key to the entire surface rubbing down with fine glasspaper and then using a tacky rag, wipe over to remove all dust and grit after each coat.

Removing the dust and grit is the key to a smooth painted surface.

Using non-drip gloss

This paint has a thick consistency, like jelly, and needs no brushing out. Load the brush, and paint with vertical strokes; do not cross brush and do not try to make the paint spread. It is designed to be painted on thickly and only one coat should be necessary. This type of paint is obviously useful when painting overhead. You do not need to stir non-drip paint, but if the paint shows signs of the solvent separating, stir it to blend it in again, but for best results, leave the paint until it has assumed its jelly-like consistency again and its non-drip quality.

PAINTING WINDOWS

There will be no large flat expanses of paint here, so achieving a smooth finish is rather easier. However, as there are a lot of narrow edges and moldings where paint can accumulate, be particularly careful not to overload the brush.

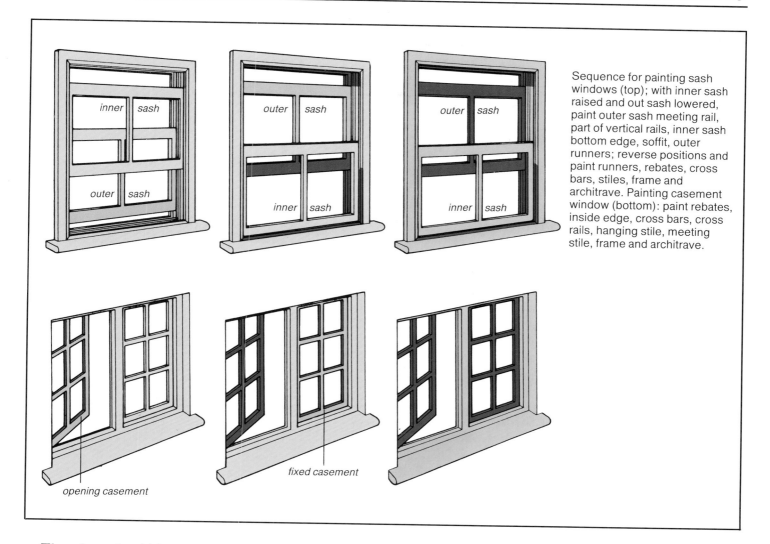

Sequence for painting sash windows (top); with inner sash raised and out sash lowered, paint outer sash meeting rail, part of vertical rails, inner sash bottom edge, soffit, outer runners; reverse positions and paint runners, rebates, cross bars, stiles, frame and architrave. Painting casement window (bottom): paint rebates, inside edge, cross bars, cross rails, hanging stile, meeting stile, frame and architrave.

The glass should be masked with masking tape or double-sided tape and newspaper. Alternatively, you can buy a metal or plastic paint shield or cut one from cardboard: hold close against the rebate where it meets the glass as you apply the paint. Carry the paint film onto the glass by about $\frac{1}{8}$in so that a water-tight seal is formed.

If spots of paint do get onto the glass, leave them to dry and then scrape off with a razor blade.

As with doors there is a sequence to follow for painting each type of window.

Sash windows Open the window, raising the lower sash almost to the top and bringing the upper sash as far down as possible. Paint as much of the upper sash as is now accessible and the bottom edge (that closes down on the frame) of the lower sash. Then move to the top of the window and paint the soffit and 2 to 3in of the outside runner on each side, being careful not to get paint on the sash cords.

Reverse the position of the sashes. Paint 2 to 3in down the inside runners at the top and the same distance up both inside and outside runners at the bottom. There is no need to paint the full length of the runners as they are protected by the tight fit of the sashes. They only need the paint at the top and the bottom for protection when the window is opened. However, it also looks better to see paint match the decor.

Paint the rebates next, applying a thin coat with a cutting-in brush and masking or shielding the glass. The cross bars and stiles come next followed by the frame and the casing.

Casement windows Fasten the window open slightly. The sequence of painting is much the same as for sash windows. Paint all the rebates and inside edges, which close against the frame, first, protecting the glass from the paint with a piece of card or firm plastic cut to an appropriate size. Move to the cross bars and the cross rails. Paint the hanging stile next and then the meeting stile. Finally paint the frame and casing.

SPECIAL PAINT EFFECTS

There are numerous patterned effects that can be created with paint. Basically, they all involve using one or more colors on top of another. The overall effect is detemined entirely by the choice of colors. Combining several shades of the same color or closely related pastels leads to a soft, gentle effect, whereas using the same painting technique but choosing contrasting bold colors will create a more dramatic finish.

Right: Ragging on; when the base coat is dry, dab on the covering coat at regular intervals with a crumpled rag.
Dragging; Using two people for large areas – as one paints vertical strips of paint, the other goes over it with a wide, dry paint brush, causing lines of the base coat to show through.

Ragging on

This looks particularly effective when a dark color is ragged onto a lighter base coat. The technique is much the same as sponging on but the result, a crinkled look, is more like that achieved with rag rolling (see page 25). Using a rag is not quite so easy as using a sponge.

Allow the base coat to dry. Dilute the color to be ragged on, if you prefer, and spoon some into a bowl. Testing the impression created by the rag in order to gain the desired effect is the most important stage of the operation.

Crumple up a piece of rag. Dab it into the paint until it is fairly saturated then press on to a piece of lining paper. If you do not like the pattern bunch up the rag again and see what impressions can be made.

When you are happy with the pattern, and the paint has been dabbed off to create the required crinkled look, press the rag gently on the wall. Raise your hand from the wall, turn it slightly and press the rag onto an adjoining area. The spaces between pressings should be kept fairly even.

As the paint runs out, the impression will fade. Refill the rag with paint, keeping it bunched as it is to continue the same print or crumpling again for a more random effect. As with sponging on, too much sponged color can be concealed by ragging on a little of the base color.

Dragging

Dragging is a popular treatment for woodwork as well as walls, and is one of the paint effects that is best achieved by two people working together. Latex or semi gloss enamel can be used on walls, semi gloss only on woodwork.

The effect is created by painting a thin glaze of color over a base coat then using a dry brush to drag off this color, allowing the base color to show through: the result is finely graduating lines. They can be dragged vertically or horizontally, even one on top of the other, but with woodwork the dragging looks better when it follows the grain of the wood.

Dilute the color to be dragged at least 50:50. Mix enough to drag a complete wall. Mix any remainder into the next batch. Do not try to join two batches in the middle of one wall.

The work progresses in strips about 2ft wide, one person brushing on the color, the second person dragging it off while it is still wet (remember that latex dries more quickly than enamels).

Brush the paint on thinly and evenly, so that it completely covers the base color. When a complete strip has been painted, one person moves on to paint the second while the other drags the first strip.

Hold the dragging brush (a proper one is expensive – a long-bristled wide brush will do) firmly and draw it steadily down through the wet paint. Your touch should be firm but light. Wipe the brush on rags after two or three strokes so that it does not become so loaded with paint that it puts it on rather than takes it off. Relax the grip at the end of a stroke – at the bottom of the wall, round light switches and other obstacles as this is where paint tends to build up.

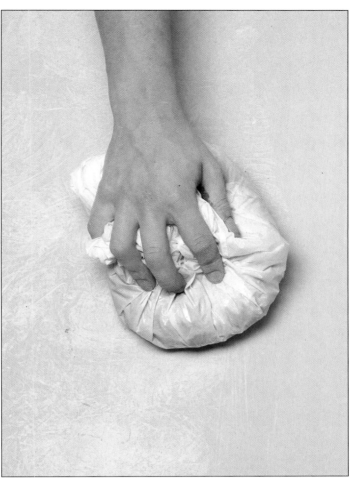

Bag graining is best carried out by two people; one covers the base coat in 2ft wide strips with thinned graining coat, while the other presses a plastic bag, half filled with rags, into overlapping areas of the wet paint.

The edge of each strip of paint being brushed on must remain wet if the strip next to it is to merge properly. Any build up of drying paint between strips will be obvious and will ruin the delicate effect. The painter should start applying the second strip while the dragger works on the first; the dragger follows the painter along the wall.

It may not be necessary to have two people working on woodwork as the area to be covered is, obviously, not so large and enamels do not dry as quickly as latex paint.

Bag graining

This crushed velvet type of finish using two colors is best achieved with two people working in tandem. The graining coat is diluted as for dragging (again, latex or enamel) and a sufficient quantity must always be mixed for a wall: (a slight variation in color between walls will not show but on one wall it will).

The bag for the graining is simply a lightweight plastic bag half-filled with rags and secured by a knot, held nearest to the palm. Paint on the diluted graining coat exactly as for dragging, in strips about 2ft wide,

thinly and evenly to cover the base coat.

The person doing the graining can start work on the top half of the first strip while the painter works on the bottom half. There will be little danger of paint drying too quickly if this rhythm is maintained.

Press the graining bag onto the surface, lift and place on an adjoining area. Wipe excess paint off the bag. Overlap the bag impressions slightly to create the crushed and crinkled impression. If the grained coat of paint appears too dominant, go over it again with the bag, continually wiping off the excess paint with a rag.

Rag rolling

A particularly attractive and impressive finish for walls, although it is more difficult to apply. Satin enamel is best for this, resulting in a wrinkled effect with a soft sheen rather like silk. The patterning is more marked than that achieved with the other techniques and there is greater surface variety.

The process is similar to bag graining. The top coat of color (diluated with white spirit) is painted over the base coat in strips 2ft wide by one person, then rolled

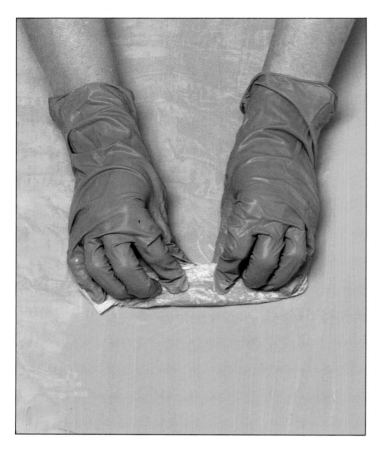

Rag rolling; after coating the base coat with thinned latex paint, roll the rag into a sausage shape and, wearing rubber gloves, roll it in overlapping strips over the surface. Re-roll the rag when it becomes soaked with paint.

Marbling; after painting glaze and light veins over the base coat, add darker veins before softening with a dry brush.

off with a bunched up rag by the second person. Make sure there is a good supply of rags cut to about 1ft square before starting work.

Roll the rag into a sausage shape about 6in wide. Hold between two hands (wear rubber gloves), then roll up the painted strip, lifting off the paint to reveal the base coat. When the rag becomes paint-soaked, re-roll it to produce a clean surface or use a new rag.

Overlap the vertically-rolled 6in strips slightly. Leave an edge of about 2in next to the second strip of paint being applied so that the rag rolling can run right up the join, making the two painted areas merge completely.

Apply the top coat of paint with vertical strokes from the top to the bottom of the wall and rag-roll the paint off working from the baseboard upward.

Marbling

True marbling is a highly skilled technique and amateurs can really only aim for the faster impressionistic finish, which still imitates the broken color finish of the real thing. Study some examples before starting, to see how the veins interlink and change direction. The process involves several stages and some specialist equipment is necessary: an artist's brush and artist's oil colors in raw umber and black.

Use enamel paint for the base colors.

First, a diluted glaze of white enamel tinted with a little black artist's paint is applied over a base coat of white and sponged off (see Sponging Off and Bag Graining for details). Allow to dry thoroughly.

Apply veins to this surface by painting on, with an artist's brush, strokes of gray-brown color (a mix of black and raw umber). The paint strokes should be fidgety and form a pattern of diagonals, one stroke meeting another. Sponge lightly to remove excess paint and soften the lines by stroking a paintbrush or a feather along them. Mix up a darker gray and working diagonally paint in some fine darker veins, joining them to the original ones. Sponge the veins to soften them and agitate the sponge on the areas between the veins to imitate the spots of color in real marble.

Soften the whole effect again with a dry paintbrush, drawing it along each diagonal. Repeat until the effect is suitably softened.

Leave the surface to dry and then paint in some veins and blotches of diluted white satin enamel paint. For a richer effect, repeat the veining with a second color that can be found in real marble.

To achieve a sheen like marble, varnish with matt or satin coat varnish. When dry, sprinkle over French chalk and rub off with a duster.

Sponging on

This is the simplest of techniques, creating a speckled effect. Two or more colors can be used. Having applied a solid base coat of color to the entire surface, the other colors are dabbed on to it, using a natural sponge for the best effect. The base coat will always be the dominant color.

The base coat can be either latex or semi gloss. Using flat latex produces the softest build up of color, but enamel is preferable in a bathroom. Allow to dry for 24 hours.

The paint to be sponged on can be used as it is or thinned for a more delicate, translucent effect. Thin latex with water, oil based semi gloss with white spirit, 50:50 to start with, adding more thinners if preferred.

Spoon a little of the paint into a bowl. Dampen the sponge with water and squeeze it out. Press the flat side into the paint to absorb most of it. Test the effect on a piece of lining paper pressing on the sponge. The impression may not be very effective at this point but as the paint is dabbed off, a general speckled effect will appear.

Now move to the prepared wall. Dab the sponge on, being careful not to skid across the surface. The speckled look will lessen as the paint runs out. Refill the sponge with paint, test as before and continue. When the wall/room is finished, leave the sponged-on color to dry for 24 hours. A second color can be sponged on in exactly the same way after this time.

Try to apply the second color so that it fills the gaps between the first set of sponge marks, slightly overlapping to create a random effect.

If it appears that too much color has been sponged on, this is easily remedied by sponging some of the base color over the sponged color when it has dried.

Sponging off

This is identical to bag graining except that the paint is sponged away with a natural sponge rather than grained with a bag of rags. See Bag Graining for further details.

Stenciling

A patterned paint effect for walls, floors and furniture, the designs should be kept simple, combining two or more basic patterns for a more intricate effect. Two or three colors is also the best combination, applied on a neutral background.

Ready-made stencils can be bought from artist's suppliers and some decorator's merchants. Originals can be cut very easily by drawing the design on ordinary paper and tracing it on to acetate paper. This is the best stencil material to use as it can be wiped clean and used many times. Use a utility knife for the actual cutting. If the stencil is to be used over a large area, it is sensible to cut several at the same time. They can then be compared to make sure they have been identically cut.

If several stencils form part of the pattern, each being painted a different color, cut them all and line them up in advance, making holes which can be matched up when they are put on the wall.

Mark guidelines for the width and height of the stencil on the wall in chalk so that as the stencil is moved along the wall it matches the previous pattern exactly. Fix it in position with masking tape. Apply the paint with a special stencil brush, stippling it through the holes in the stencil card. Leave to harden for a few minutes, then release the card and place it in the next position. Continue until this stencil is complete. Allow to dry completely before using the second stencil and the second color on top, matching it up by the registration holes as was done when the stencils were originally cut. Color in this stencil in exactly the same way as the first.

Stenciling is best carried out with enamel paint, as it dries quickly. However, on floors or furniture some protection will be necessary. When the paint is completely dry, use polyurethane varnish, in several coats on floors, and flat, satin coat or high gloss finish as preferred.

Stencilling; buy ready-made stencils or cut them from acetate sheet, and fix them to the surface with masking tape.

Apply the paint with a stippling motion using a stencilling brush which has a broad, flat end for even coverage.

USING TEXTURED PAINT

Walls and ceilings that are in bad condition, that is, they have been prepared properly but are covered with cracks and holes that have been filled and the surface is impossible to make perfectly smooth, are best covered with a textured finish. Textured paint is easy to apply and is much quicker to use than textured paper. Its only drawback is that it is difficult to strip, should you want a change in the future. But used judiciously, this should not be necessary.

Surfaces to be textured must be sound. Although the paint conceals defects very efficiently it will not adhere to unstable surfaces, to paper or to polystyrene tiles. It cannot be used to cover areas that should be replastered and a recommended stabilizing primer should be used on porous or powdery backings. If being applied over paintwork, this should be sanded down to provide a key.

If the background color is very deep, it is a good idea to paint on one coat of white before using the textured paint. This, of course, is not necessary if the textured paint is to be painted anyway. It can be used directly on ceramic tiles if the grout lines are filled in and a PVA adhesive primer applied first.

The paint does tend to spatter and, apart from protective clothing, goggles, a facemask and protection for the head are advised.

Tools for patterning
Textured paint is not just a cover-up; it can be patterned in several ways with accessories or homemade tools and may be preferred to a flat finish. Large-toothed combs cut from a piece of firm plastic (an old ice cream carton, for example) can be swept over the wall to create swirling designs or used in short, straight lines to create structured squares. The teeth could be cut raggedly for a random effect or evenly for a measured pattern effect.

A sponge in a plastic bag pressed onto the wet paint will create small swirls. The accessory tools available include a swirlbrush and patterned rollers with diagonal, diamond and bark-effect designs cut in their surfaces.

Painting
Of the two types of textured paint available, the powdered version dries too slowly for patterning, but the ready-mixed variety can also be patterned successfully and needs no overpainting.

Use either a roller (not a patterned one) or a large whitewash brush to apply the paint. As only one coat

1 After applying textured paint, creating swirls in the surface with a comb.
2 Creating a block pattern with a piece of batten; sand off sharp points when dry.
3 Forming a regular diamond pattern with a contoured roller.
4 With a coarse foam roller, creating an overall stippled effect.

is used it must be thick enough to conceal any defects and provide a good thick base for patterning. Work in bands up and down the wall (or across the ceiling working from the window towards the opposite wall) until the whole surface is covered. Pattern this area before painting the next wall.

Patterning
There will usually be plenty of time to pattern the paint before it dries but check the manufacturer's instructions. If in doubt, and a structured, more detailed pattern is planned, pattern each strip as you finish painting, being careful to match the pattern from strip to strip.

Random patterns do not need this consideration and are quick to effect. In fact, applying the paint with a plain foam-covered roller creates a small stipple effect and needs no patterning. Brush strokes are usually too random and need some smoothing out with a roller or patterning tool.

When the paint has dried, knock off any sharp projections, especially on walls.

Maintenance
The powdered textured paint finish will need painting. Both this finish and the ready-mixed variety are easily maintained by repainting. The surface should be cleaned of dust and dirt by detergent and water applied with a paintbrush.

• CHECKPOINT •

Graining wood
The purpose of graining is to make a plain surface look like a piece of wood. The decorative element is the important thing with graining at this level, not producing a perfect copy of nature.

Color
The effect is created by spreading a colored transparent glaze over a solid base color then brushing out the glaze to acquire graining and knots.

Two shades of color look better in combination than contrasting colors, but they need not be brown. For a truly dramatic and original effect choose a color that fits the decorative scheme of the room but will stand out: shades of gray in a basically white or cream room; deep raspberry in a room of pastel pink. Green, blue, yellow, red can all look spectacular in the right setting.

The lighter of the two shades should form the base, as this will be the dominant color; the deeper shade, used to paint in the wood grain and knots, will never then appear too heavy.

Materials
The base color must have a non-porous finish so that the glaze can be worked on without being absorbed into the base. Satin enamel paint, with its mid-sheen finish, is ideal; latex can be used but should be sealed with satincoat varnish. The transparent glaze, sometimes called "scumble glaze", can be bought ready-mixed but it has to be colored: artists' oil colors offer the widest range of colors. It can be used like this but a subtler effect will be created if the glaze is diluted with white spirit and it will retain its slight sheen.

Method
The base coat must be completely dry. Brush on the glaze with a small decorator's brush. Use either an old decorator's brush with clumps of bristles cut away or a comb made from plastic or cardboard with unevenly spaced teeth to mark the grain.

Drag the brush or comb along the surface, keeping a loose wrist, so as to achieve gently rippling lines rather than

dead straight ones. Soften the grain by stroking the surface with a soft-bristled brush, following the line of the grain.

Paint in the heartwood, joining the graining and curving it, using an artist's brush. Having a piece of wood to copy will make this stage much easier. Make knots in the "wood" by dipping a rag-covered finger into the glaze and then pressing it to the surface, turning it at the same time.

When the base coat is dry, applying the colored glaze with a small decorator's brush.

Marking the grain in the glaze with a cardboard comb.

Softening the grain by brushing lightly with a soft bristle brush.

Painting in the heartwood with a fine artist's brush.

Making knots with a rag-covered finger dipped in glaze.

CHAPTER 3

COVERING WALLS AND CEILINGS

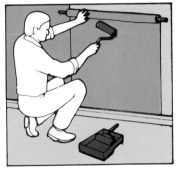

With a tremendous variety of wall coverings to choose from, it is essential that you plan your scheme ahead, making sure that you choose the most appropriate covering for your particular needs. Once you have chosen a wall covering, which may be made from paper, paper-backed fabric, cork, woven grass, flock or glass fiber, for example, you will need to know how much to buy, how to apply it, and which adhesive to use.

This chapter tells you exactly how to calculate amounts, how to hang regular wallpaper, and the more specialist types. It also includes papering a stairwell and ceiling, with all the practical know-how required for the non-specialist home-decorator to achieve impressive results time after time.

WALL COVERINGS

Decorative wall coverings can be applied to any flat surface in the home. This includes not only all walls but also ceilings and, for example, the panels in wooden doors. All that is required is that the surface is properly prepared (see pages 9–13).

There are various types of wallpaper, not to mention fabric finishes, and certain types are obviously more appropriate for use in different rooms. Nearly all come in a standard width of 20 or 22in and some are 27in wide. Bathrooms and kitchens can pose a problem with condensation, however good the ventilation in the rooms may be. If the walls are not smooth enough simply to be painted, a lining paper could be used to disguise the unevenness. Vinyl emulsion would then provide a washable finish in the same way as vinyl wallpaper.

The more expensive hand-printed papers and fabric finishes are best restricted to areas such as living rooms, dining rooms and bedrooms. Hallways tend to suffer wear and tear simply because they are thoroughfares and they also include the most inaccessible part of a house for papering: the stairwell, so choose a covering that is straightforward to hang.

Concealing a poor surface

● **Lining paper** is used on bare walls that are to be painted and it also gives the perfect face on which to hang decorative wallpapers, evening out any small imperfections in the surface. It comes in several weights – heavier paper being useful in hiding very uneven surfaces and as a base for heavy wallcoverings. Used under paint, hang lining paper vertically as for wallpaper; and under wall coverings, hang it horizontally around the room so that the butt joins do not coincide with those of the wallcovering.

With unbacked fabric wall coverings, it is essential to use lining paper and paint it in a color to match the top covering so that the whiteness of the paper does not show through the top fabric wall covering. Whereas standard wallpaper paste is normally sufficient for hanging lining paper, with a heavy decorative covering it may be necessary to use heavy-duty paste so that the weight of the covering does not pull the lining paper from the wall.

● **Woodchip (ingrain) papers** is a relief lining-type paper coated with small wood-chips then covered with another sheet of paper to seal in the chips. There are various textures of woodchip according to the size of the chips. Colored wood-chip can be bought but it is generally used as a lining on walls with minor imperfections and is then painted. It is hung vertically like ordinary wallpaper.

● **High relief papers** are particularly heavy coverings, some designed to be painted over, others already finished, which are very efficient in concealing the defects in cracked and uneven surfaces. One made from thick paper, is embossed on both sides; another is made from cotton fibers; another is made from vinyl. These patterns come in a range of designs, from sculpturally classic to geometric effects, and are suitable for different styles of home.

Many of these papers are used to cover the lower part of a wall (the dado) (if not the whole wall) where they are most likely to suffer scuff marks.

● **Embossed covering** with a flat paper back comes plain, to be painted, or ready decorated, and includes finishes such as tile and brick simulations. The edges as well as the ends of each length need to be trimmed before hanging, using a straight-edge and sharp trimming knife.

Coverings for decorative effect

● **Surface-printed papers** are standard wall coverings which vary in thickness and the thinner ones may need care in handling to prevent tearing. Standard papers are made in a vast selection of printed patterns, but are not washable.

Hand-printed papers are more expensive, and do not all come in the standard width. Some are also sold with edges that need trimming.

● **Washable papers** as the name implies, have a thin plastic (PVA) coating, which can be washed; ideal for use in areas such as the kitchen and bathroom.

Some washable papers come ready-pasted. These are cut to length, where each length is soaked in a special water trough then positioned on to the wall. They are easy to hang but, like vinyls, need special paste where any overlapping is unavoidable as the paper will not stick to itself.

● **Borders** come in various widths from about 2 to 6in, and are often color co-ordinated with a wide range of wallpapers. Some borders have straight edges on both sides while others may have either one or two decoratively cut edges.

Use a border at any height: around the top of the wall, butting the ceiling; at base level, continuing around door-frames; at about 3ft up the wall to create a dado effect; around the edge of the ceiling; or simply around the features that deserve particular definition – a recessed fireplace for example. Borders can be used very effectively around contrasting wall-papered panels in rooms, halls and staircases.

TYPES OF WALL COVERING

As alternatives to paint, there are many other finishes, both practical and pretty, that can be used in decorating the home.

Vinyl wall coverings

Vinyl coverings are washable and particularly durable. The vinyl layer, fused with a printed pattern, is backed with paper and is no more difficult to hang than ordinary paper. The only slight complication is that paper will not stick to vinyl so, where overlapping is unavoidable, a special adhesive must be used. Also, to prevent mold growing in the paper behind the impervious vinyl layer, a fungicidal size and paste must be used. The paste is applied to the covering as with ordinary paper.

Expanded (blown) vinyl wall coverings

These are thicker than ordinary vinyl and are especially suitable in rooms such as kitchens or bathrooms where condensation might be a problem. They must be left to soak after pasting and extra paste on the wall will be needed at joins. All joins are butted and rolled, but pattern-free papers can be joined like furnishing hessian (see page 38) where the edges are overlapped and then cut through for a matching butt join.

Flock wall coverings

These are made by sticking the fibers of a fabric or wood to paper, creating a raised velvety pile effect, usually in two-tone coloring. Care must be taken not to get any paste on the front of the paper. They do not clean well. However, vinyl flocks are both tough and washable. It does not matter if paste gets on the surface of these as it can be sponged off. Flock paper is hung like other textile wallcoverings.

Hessian

Hessian can be bought either paper-backed ready for hanging or unbacked, as a furnishing fabric. The paper-backed variety – usually in 35in or 36in wide rolls – is by far the easier to hang and can be treated like any other paper-backed textile wall covering. It comes in several shades and can also be painted over.

Furnishing hessian comes in broad rolls, and is usually sold by the yard. Being unbacked the condition and color of the wall behind are of importance. Always line the walls, as the old color could show through the weave. Check that furnishing hessian is color-fast, shrink-resistant and moth-proof.

Felt and suede

Coverings rich in color, felt and imitation suede are heavy (usually paper-backed) fabrics made from dyed compressed wool, and are produced in rolls 28in wide. With the wall pasted, the felt is pressed on from the bottom upwards, a paint roller being used to smooth it into place. It can be butt-joined or overlapped and trimmed but the joins should not be rolled or they will appear unnaturally flattened. Roll the whole length of the felt instead.

Grasscloth

This luxurious material is made by weaving natural grasses with a fine cotton weft. Not a hardwearing covering. So long as the paste is kept off the grass itself, it is not difficult to hang. A special ready-mixed paste is needed, applied to the back of the covering, not the wall. The seams should not be rolled, or the effect will be flattened.

Rolls are normally about 36in wide and may be sold by the yard.

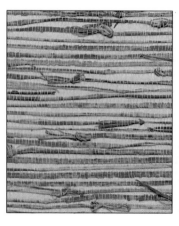

More unusual wall coverings. Top left to right: furnishing hessian, foil with matching border; Bottom left to right: grass cloth and flock.

Striped and floral patterned wallpapers with a selection of contrasting floral borders in different widths and styles.

The method of hanging varies; with many, the paste is applied to the wall and seams are usually butt-joined, though some can be overlapped and cut (see page 38).

Never use water on these coverings as this can cause severe shrinkage. Dust down regularly with a brush to clean and remove any stains with a dry upholstery cleaner. Should an accident occur, this is best treated immediately, otherwise it becomes more difficult to remove a dried-in stain.

Foamed polyethylene

This unique wall covering is ideal for kitchens and bathrooms. It is made from foamed polyethylene (with no paper backing) and, being warm, helps to reduce condensation. It is extremely light to handle and easy to hang. It comes in standard-sized rolls and in a wide variety of designs and colors.

Fabric

Lengths of furnishing fabric can be used as a covering for walls but should be reserved for areas where the effect can be appreciated and where cleaning is not a problem. If the fabric has a wool content, make sure it has been mothproofed. Vacuuming is the best method of cleaning.

The fabric can be stuck directly to the pasted wall or stapled to a series of battens around the room at ceiling and baseboard height.

To offer some protection against absorbing dust, fabric wall coverings can be sprayed with a proprietary dust repellent. Such fabrics may be cleaned by lightly sponging after vacuuming.

Cork-faced fabric

Thin veneers of natural cork stuck onto a paper backing make an interesting textured wall covering that is warm to the touch and subtle in tone. Some types have the colored backing showing through for a random-patterned effect.

Great care should be taken when applying cork-faced fabric as it is relatively brittle.

Tiling on a roll

Quicker to put up, and warmer than ceramic tiles, tiling on a roll is also scrubbable, easy to hang and strips off like vinyl wall coverings, leaving its backing paper on the wall. It is a paste-the-wall type of covering and is smoothed into place with a sponge.

Textile wall coverings

There are many different patterns and effects created by fabrics and fibers being fixed to a paper backing. As with paper-backed hessian, this makes the hanging much more straightforward.

Silk cloth is probably the most expensive, and so it is sensible to take great care and not soak it with paste, or crease it.

Wool, tweed and rayon effects are no more expensive than some ordinary surface-printed papers but offer a cosier appearance. Roll widths are typically: silk, 31in; wool, 27in or 30in; tweed, 27in.

HANGING WALLPAPER

The preparation for surfaces to be papered is given in detail on pages 9 to 13. The walls must be cleaned of all grease and dirt, damaged paint or paper either stripped or repaired and cracks and holes filled and smoothed. Unstable (powdery) surfaces must be sealed with a primer and paint finishes sanded to provide a key for the paste.

New plaster must be left for four to six months to dry out before papering. If you want a temporary decorative finish, cover with latex paint. This allows the plaster to continue its drying out process.

The painting of all the woodwork in the room should be completely finished prior to papering. It must be allowed to harden for at least a week or any knocks will spoil it at the next stage of decorating.

The order of work in any room is: ceiling, woodwork, walls. If it is necessary to paper the ceiling with lining paper prior to painting, do this first, following the instructions on page 40. The painting of the ceiling can then be done in unison with the painting of the woodwork as it is unlikely that one will interfere with the other.

Sizing

Before hanging any paper, lining or otherwise, on any wall, the surface should be sized.

This treatment prevents the wall drawing out the moisture from the paste used to hang the paper enabling it to be slid on the wall during hanging, to form good butt joints between strips.

Size can be bought or wallpaper paste diluted with water as instructed on the packet. Apply the size with a large paintbrush and allow to dry.

If a fungicidal paste is needed for hanging then a fungicidal size must also be used.

Equipment

Pasting table The ideal size is 6ft × 2ft but any clean kitchen or work table will do.

Pasting brush A large, clean paintbrush, at least 4in wide, is best.

Pasting bucket A 1 gal plastic bucket will do. Tie a piece of string across the top, from one end of the handle to the other, for resting the brush when not in use and scraping off excess paste.

Scissors Paperhanger's scissors have extra-long blades but a large pair of household scissors can be used instead.

Paperhanging brush This is a flat-handled brush with long bristles, used for smoothing down the paper once it has been pasted to the wall. It will squeeze all the air out from behind the paper and prevent air pockets or bubbles forming. A sponge should be used with washable papers.

Seam roller With either a wooden or plastic roller, this is used to flatten the joins between the lengths of paper ensuring they stick.

Plumbline A plumbline or spirit level that can be used vertically is needed to ensure that the first length of paper is hung straight.

•CHECKPOINT•

Pasting wallpaper

Mix the paste with water in a plastic bucket or bowl. Having cut several lengths of paper, place these face down on the pasting table, with the first length on top. To allow the paste to soak in (some heavyweights need about 10 minutes), paste several sheets before you start hanging. Allow about three minutes soaking for the average weight of paper. This not only allows the paper to become more supple and easier to hang but also to expand to its fullest extent. If paper is hung too quickly it will expand on the walls and, being constricted by the paper on each side, will either spread out at the joins or bubbles will form in the middle.

Spread the paste over the entire surface of the paper. Position the paper so that one edge runs along the far side of the table, one end square with one end of the table, the other overhanging and retained by string looped round the table legs. Stroke the paste along the paper, then the center, being careful to paste right up to the edge away from you and the end. When this part of the paper is fully pasted, pull the top strip towards the near edge of the table and repeat the procedure. Fold the paper back on itself, pasted sides together, move it along the table to hang over the edge and paste the other end. Fold this back in the same way, remove from the table and leave to soak (drape over a broom handle across two chair backs).

Always try to make the first fold the longer one, indicating the top of the paper – which can be marked lightly with pencil when cutting it.

Folding the pasted paper back on itself to prevent it from drying out; support the hanging end in a loop of string.

Stepladder To reach the top of the wall. A stool or strong box may be easier to work from, in which case an apron with a large pocket will be useful as there will be nowhere to rest the hanging brush and scissors while the paper is being manoeuvred.

Paste

In general the heavier the paper, the thicker the paste should be.

There are two types of cellulose paste one for lightweight papers, the other for heavyweights. Certain types are suitable for all coverings and are mixed, to be thicker or thinner.

The paste used to hang vinyls and washable papers must contain a fungicide to prevent a growth of mold behind the paper. Fungicidal paste should also be used if, during preparation, the wall was treated for mold, or showed signs of damp. Use a fungicidal size (or diluted fungicidal paste) also.

Certain special wall coverings (see page 38) need particularly strong adhesive and this will be given in the manufacturer's instructions for hanging. Ready-pasted papers, of course, need no further pasting.

How much paper to buy

Most wallpapers are sold in rolls 33ft long and 27in wide. Measure around the room and if the door or window space is particularly large (wide French windows for example with little wall space above) make an allowance for this in the measurement; if not, ignore them. The number of drops of paper needed is this figure divided by the width of the paper. To estimate how many "drops" can be cut from each roll.

• Measure the height of the room from baseboard to ceiling.

• Divide this figure into the length of the roll. For example, in a room that is 8ft high, four lengths can be cut from a single roll. The number of rolls needed to paper the whole room is the number of drops needed divided by four.

These calculations must take into account pattern matching and pattern repeats. Matching a pattern always creates waste and this must be allowed for. It cannot be measured absolutely accurately, so if the pattern repeat is large it is probably best to allow an extra roll of paper. Never buy too few rolls: to be certain of the colors being the same on every roll of paper they must all come from the same batch. If you run short, an extra roll may not match perfectly. To be on the safe side, always check batch numbers when buying your wallpaper.

Pattern matching and repeats

Measure the height of the wall for the first drop and cut a piece of paper this length plus 2in top and bottom for trimming. Lay this sheet on the pasting table face up, and unroll the paper from which the second length is to be cut next to it.

Slide the roll along until the pattern matches (there will be more waste at the top) and cut it to match the first length. Follow this procedure for each length of paper, always matching the new length to the one before it.

Some papers have a pattern that matches straight across the wall, others have what is called a "drop pattern". With drop match papers, alternate lengths begin half a repeat further on the roll, so that length one and all odd-numbered lengths will match, and all even-numbered lengths will match length two.

Pattern matching sounds more complicated than it is in practice: with the pattern to look at, matching becomes obvious. You may save on wastage by cutting lengths from two rolls of paper alternately.

Hanging lining paper

If lining paper is to be painted over it can be hung vertically like any other paper. If it is being used as a backing for a decorative paper, it should be hung horizontally.

The finish does not have to be quite so perfect, as any mistakes will be hidden; a slight gap between joins, for instance, will not matter, but an overlap between two strips will show.

Cut the paper to cover the length of the wall, allowing about 2in top and bottom for trimming. Paste and fold the paper concertina fashion and start at the top of the wall.

Do not paper around corners. Allow about ½in to go over onto the adjacent wall and make a butt joint when papering that wall. Trim close to doors and windows. Cut around light switches, sockets and wall lights as explained below. Finish one wall before going on to the next.

Hanging lining paper; fold it into a narrow concertina for ease of handling and hang in horizontal strips, starting at the top.

Where to start papering

If there are four flat walls, start on the wall with the door. Work around the room from the opening side of the door, ending by hanging the final sheet of paper behind the door.

In a room with a chimney breast, hang the first drop in the center of the breast and work back on each side towards the doorway. By this method, any pattern loss (final length meeting first length) will be in the least conspicuous part of the room.

Finding the vertical

When starting from the door, measure out at the top of the frame about 1in less than the width of the paper. Make a pencil mark. If using a spirit level with a vertical bubble, put it to this mark and draw a continuous line down the wall: extend it using a long straight-edged batten. If using a plumbline, drop it from this point and make pencil marks at intervals down the line, then correct them using a straight-edged batten.

This gives the true vertical on that wall: the first length of paper is placed to this line and waste trimmed at the edge of the door frame. Check that at no point does the distance from the line to the door measure more than the width of the paper. If it does, draw a second vertical slightly closer to the door, so that there is always paper to be trimmed.

If the first length of paper is to be hung from a corner of the room, trim the waste to allow ¾in to overlap the corner on to the adjoining wall.

To find the vertical on a chimney breast, measure the width and divide in half to find the center point. Mark this and measure back 13½in or half the width of your roll. Mark the vertical from this point and paste the first length of paper in the center of the breast, with one edge to this line.

Hanging straight drops

Position the stepladder alongside the starting point. Carry the folded paper to the wall, hold it by the top edge so that the fold falls away and place it to the marked vertical line, aligning it with the vertical edge of the paper.

Smooth the paper onto the wall at the top with the paperhanging brush. Brush it straight down the center of the paper then with outward strokes, pressing any air bubbles out towards the edges. Align the edge of the paper with the marked vertical all the way down the wall, smoothing the paper and using the bristles of the brush to work it into the ceiling and baseboard at top and bottom, making a crease line.

Crease the overlaps at top and bottom with the back of the scissors, gently peel the paper back trim then smooth back into position.

At sides of doorframes and windows, brush the paper into the angle to make a crease. Define this with a pencil line or scissors, peel back, cut away the excess and smooth down again. At the corners of frames, cut diagonally into the paper at this point. If the cut is slightly too long, do not worry: when the paper is smoothed flat, the cut will not show.

With light switches and sockets, first turn off the electricity supply. Smooth the paper down to the obstruction and then cut a cross in the paper over the center of it. Mark the outline of the switch or socket and extend the cross cuts back just past these lines. Trim the excess and smooth down.

With flush outlets, turn off the power at the mains, loosen the screws holding the faceplate of the outlet, then smooth the paper underneath and screw the facing back, hiding the cut edge of the paper. Follow the same procedure for wall-light fittings always

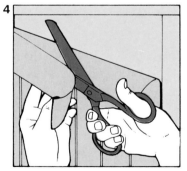

1 After marking the starting position on the wall, hanging a plumb line to one side of the mark and drawing a line through the mark.
2 Hanging the first length of paper in a corner; position the outer edge along the marked line and brush into the wall/ceiling angle.

3 Smoothing the paper onto the wall, from the center outwards to avoid trapping any air pockets, using a hanging brush.
4 After creasing the paper into the wall/ceiling angle with the back of the scissors; pulling it away from the wall to trim the top edge.

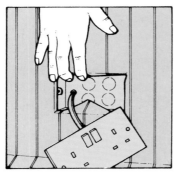

After making angled cuts in the paper; creasing the flaps along the edges of an electrical outlet with the back of the scissors.

After removing the circuit fuse, tucking the trimmed flaps within the perimeter of the plate; trim foil paper along the creases.

width, plus ¾in. Paste the paper, allow to soak then hang into the corner, smoothing the excess onto the adjoining wall. Find the true vertical on this wall, using a plumbline or spirit level, at a distance from the corner to match the offcut paper. Paste this to the wall, taking it right into the corner.

Chimney breasts create both internal and external corners. The center of the chimney breast will already be papered. Measure from here to the side of the breast and add on ¾in to take the paper round the corner onto the side. Paste the paper onto the wall, butting it to the piece already in position and smooth the excess around the corner. Find the true vertical. The width of paper on the side of the chimney breast should cover the overlap from the front, but be set slightly back from the edge, and continue into and around the internal corner by ¾in. Continue as for internal corners. With window reveals, paper the insides of the reveal first, overlapping onto the main wall by ½in. The paper on the main wall should be trimmed to fall just short of the edge but covering the overlap to give a neat finish.

removing the shades and bulbs first for safety.

The drop of paper abutting a mantelpiece should be trimmed flush with the top then cut in around the sides, following the moldings.

Chimney breasts and recessed windows both create extra angles to paper around.

On an internal corner measure into the corner from the last-hung drop and cut a length of paper to this

1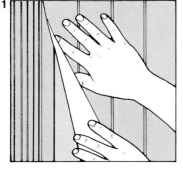

2

1

2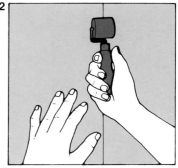

3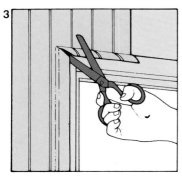

4

3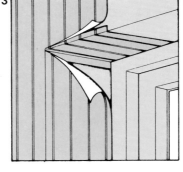

4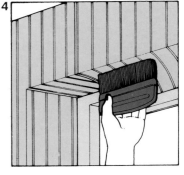

1 Papering an internal corner; hang the first length to turn the corner by ¾in and hang the second with its edge in the angle.
2 Papering an external corner; hang the paper on the face of a chimney breast to wrap round the corner, and overlap with the strip on the side.

3 After trimming wallpaper to overlap a door frame by 1in; making diagonal cuts ¼in beyond the frame at the corners.
4 Smoothing the paper into the angle of the frame before creasing into the angle; pulling away from the wall and trimming.

1 Tearing the paper above and below a windowsill or any similar obstruction to make the join less noticeable; take care as wet paper tears very easily.
2 Using a wallpaper edge roller to ensure a smooth butt join between lengths; do not use on embossed wallcoverings.

3 Papering the corner of a recess; hang an offcut to lap up the wall and down the recess and cut the length along the top of the recess.
4 Hanging the second length of paper; hang from the wall/ceiling angle, smooth under the recess and trim against the frame angle.

HANGING SPECIAL WALL COVERS

The normal way to hang wallpaper is to paste each length and press it onto the wall, working from top to bottom, butt-joining the lengths and rolling the joins. With many special wall coverings there is some variation to this method. The prime consideration is usually to avoid smearing adhesive on the front of the wall covering. It cannot easily be washed off and will undoubtedly leave a noticeable mark.

Textile wall coverings

The coverings that have a textile finish but are paper-backed can be easier to hang than ordinary wallpaper. Most, but not all of them (check the manufacturer's instructions) are hung with a heavy-duty pre-mixed adhesive which is applied to the wall.

Paste one width at a time. Do not stretch the covering but smooth it on from top to bottom, using a wide paint roller to dispel any air pockets. Butt-join the lengths, being careful to avoid paste stains. Do not seam-roll the joins or you may flatten the pile.

High relief papers

The basic approach is as with ordinary wallpaper. Paste the back of the paper, being careful to get paste into the indentations and leave to soak for 10 to 15 minutes to become supple. Butt-join the lengths but do not flatten the joins with a roller; use a paperhanger's brush instead.

To reduce the thickness where overlapping occurs (in corners), feather the edge that is underneath by tearing it straight down. Flatten this rough edge with a roller and paste the adjoining length over it.

Because the wall covering is heavy, the wall preparation must be thorough; loose paint will simply be pulled away. The wall must be well sized.

Heavily embossed papers have to be sponged with warm water prior to pasting with a special glue. Each length is immediately hung next to each other. This can make pattern matching difficult at corners, where the walls are out of line. Overlapping is impossible.

Hessian

Unbacked hessian as opposed to the paper-backed variety, is liable to shrink, so allow an extra 2in on each length. As with ordinary papering a plumbline is used to find the true vertical. Paste the wall with a heavy-duty paste applied with a paint roller.

Hang the hessian to the marked line, smoothing it from top to bottom, taking care not to stretch it. Smooth it with a clean paint roller. Overlap each

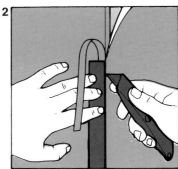
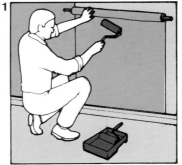
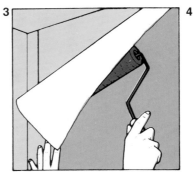
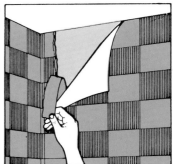

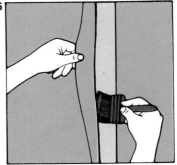

1 After applying paste to the wall with a roller, smoothing the unbacked fabric onto the wall with a clean roller.
2 Cutting along the middle of an overlapping join between lengths before peeling off the offcuts and refixing.
3 Smoothing the fabric into a corner; wrap the first length around the corner, overlap the second, cut through the overlap and refix.

4 Papering a corner with a relief wallcovering; tear along the turned length edge roll the feathered edge and overlap the next length.
5 After rolling unbacked hessian onto a pole right side inwards, hanging it on the pasted wall in overlapping lengths.
6 After cutting through the overlap and peeling off the excess, pasting under the edges with a small brush before lightly edge-rolling.

length by about 1in and leave to dry. This allows time for any shrinkage before trimming.

Using a straight-edge and sharp knife, trim at top and bottom. Cut through both layers at the center of each join. Remove the waste strips, peel back the edges and re-paste the wall. Press the edges into place to achieve a perfectly matched butt-join.

•CHECKPOINT•

Papering a stairwell

A rather complicated system of ladders, staging planks and boxes is needed to gain access to a stairwell. But stairwells vary in design and the system will have to be structured to suit the location.

Basically, you will need a long ladder placed on the stairs and leaning against the head wall. Wrap the ends of the ladder with cloths so that they do not damage the wall. Position a stepladder on the half-landing, leaning against and facing out from the well wall. If there is no carpet, this ladder can be wedged firmly in place by a length of wood screwed to the floor against it. If this is not possible, secure the ladder by jamming a length of wood between it and the next flight of stairs.

Place a stool or strong box at the top of this short flight and lay a staging board from it back to the stepladder. Another board can then be positioned at right-angles to this one, and supported by it, running back to the long ladder. If the gap is more than 5ft use two boards for strength.

Lash the boards to the ladder rungs using strong rope; it is preferable to bolt the boards to the rungs of a ladder, or attach two stout battens to the underside, spaced so they straddle a rung. (If you have rented the boards, however, you will not be able to drill bolt holes.)

It is advisable not to work alone when papering a stairwell. Quite apart from the fact that an accident is more likely, the lengths of paper needed can be extensive (often up to 19ft) and will be much heavier. Heavier papers are more likely to tear and it is useful to have a second person to support the folded length of paper.

Start papering at the longest drop, where the well wall meets the head wall. Find the true vertical with spirit level or plumbline and pencil in the line, allowing the first length of paper to turn ½in round the corner onto the adjoining head wall. Measure up and find the vertical on the head wall as well.

Measure up and cut the paper to length. If using decorative paper, measure up for the second piece, pattern-match it against the first piece from the top and cut to length. Remember to continue matching the pattern for each length of paper.

Paste the paper, fold concertina style, allow to soak for the recommended time and then walk onto the platform with the drop draped over your arm. Unfold the top piece and brush onto the wall; the folds will unfold as the paper is smoothed out onto the wall, controlled by your helper just below you. Keep the edge against the

After nailing battens to the underside of the scaffold board to prevent slipping; lashing it to the ladder rung.

Carrying a length of paper, folded into a concertina, over one arm to leave the other arm free for hanging.

pencilled vertical, brush well into the corner and flatten down the ½in overlap.

Continue papering the well wall, butting the joins and working back along the staging board to the half-landing. When this wall is finished, with ½in overlapping at the other end on to the adjoining wall, remove the boards and ladders. Paper the head wall from a stepladder on the landing.

It may be easier to hang the first drop (in the far corner) from the staging boards but because of the ladders, it will not be possible to decorate the whole wall from there.

Decorate the wall at the other end of the stairwell last — the easiest to reach. Work from the stepladder on the half-landing and the stool or box on the upper landing.

Nailing a batten to the stair tread to secure the foot of the ladder after pushing it into the tread/riser angle.

After securing the top edge, brushing the paper onto the wall while an assistant supports the weight.

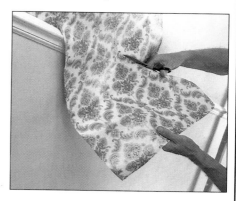

Trimming the bottom of the length to overlap a dado rail before creasing into the angle and cutting along the crease.

PAPERING A CEILING

Papering a ceiling may seem like a daunting task, but – given the correct access to the surface – there is no reason why one person alone should not be able to make a professional job; the techniques are similar to papering a wall.

To reach the ceiling you can make a "walkway" from two stepladders with a staging board between them, or rent special decorator's trestles, which enable you to comfortably span a room at the correct working height.

It is best to hang the paper across the ceiling working back from the window so you are not in your own shadow. Measure out from the window wall the width of the paper less ½in. Stretch a stringline across the ceiling, fixing it with thumb tacks, then draw a pencil line along it, using a straight-edged batten. Remove the tacks and string. Alternatively, chalk the string and snap it against the ceiling to make a chalked guideline.

Cut the paper to length, allowing extra for trimming. Paste it as described on page 34, folding it concertina style with the folds not being more than 18in. Support the folded length on a roll of paper and mount the walkway. Hold the folded paper in one hand and apply the free end to the ceiling, with the edge on the pencil line. Smooth the paper into place.

Step along the platform, unloop a concertina fold, smooth it up onto the ceiling then continue along until the whole strip is hung. If the walls are to be lined or otherwise papered, smooth the extra ½in at the side of the paper onto the wall; do the same at each end. If the walls are not being papered, mark the creases and trim into the angle between ceiling and walls in the usual way. Butt the following lengths to the first one.

Where the paper covers a ceiling-mounted light fixture, cut a cross over the fixture, slot the lamp-holder through then trim around it. With a decorative ceiling rose, paper up to it, mark the molding in pencil, peel back the edge of the paper and trim to fit as closely as possible.

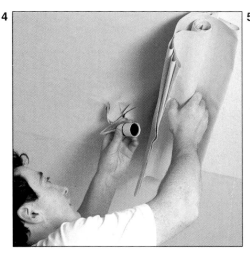

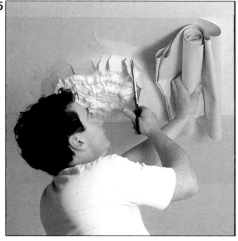

1 Snapping a chalk-line onto the ceiling, parallel to the window wall and paper-width less ½in into the room.
2 Pasting a cut length of paper; start at one end and fold the paper concertina-fashion as you progress along it.
3 Supporting the concertina on a spare roll of paper and brushing the paper onto the ceiling, parallel to the line.
4 Pulling a light fixture through a cross cut in the paper before trimming around the ceiling canopy.
5 Making a series of cuts around a molded ceiling centerpiece before hanging the rest of the length.

CHAPTER 4
FLOORS

The immense range of floor coverings widely available includes wood, vinyl, tile and carpet finishes. With the addition of some excellent synthetics the range has been made even more versatile so that spongeable carpeting can easily be laid in powder rooms and beautifully soft vinyl tiles in children's bedrooms, and so on. Before covering a floor, however, several factors need to be considered, such as practicality, cost and effect. The following pages explain all this in great detail and illustrate in step-by-step stages the professional techniques used to carry out these tasks, and at the same time, how to achieve excellent finishes that can be both practical and truly luxurious.

SANDING FLOORS

This floor treatment is in keeping with any age or style of property and costs no more than the rental of the sander, the abrasive papers and the floor seal.

Preparing the floor
Sanding floors is one of the dustiest of all decorating tasks and should be done before anything else.

Having emptied the room, go over the floor board by board to see if any repair work is needed and to prepare for sanding.

Nail heads Using a hammer and nail punch, sink all exposed nailheads to about ⅛in below the surface of the board. Any old tacks left over from a previous floorcovering should be removed with pincers.

Some boards may be secured with screws: remove these and increase the depth of their countersink holes then replace them.

Loose board If punching down the nails has no effect, drive an extra nail into each joist. If the board begins to split, secure it with countersunk screws.

Warped board This can be a problem with square-edged boards, where the edge of one board is sticking up higher than the one next to it. Do not rely on the sander but plane it smooth, following the grain of the wood. If a board is badly warped, lift it and turn it over, using extra nails to help level it.

Knots These can stand proud of the surface, especially in old boards. Either plane level or chisel off the excess. Loose knots may be stuck back in using PVA woodworking adhesive.

Gaps between boards These are not only unsightly, but extremely draughty with square-edged boards. In most cases the gaps can be filled but in an older property, where the gaps have developed over the years and are now wide and appear between virtually every board, re-laying could be the solution.

There are several methods for filling gaps, according to their size. Small gaps can be filled with a wood filler, which will expand with the boards. Work it well down into the cracks but leave it standing proud of the boards. When it is hard, sand it level and smooth. Choose a filler that is close in color to the boards.

Another filler is home-made papier-maché, based on newspaper and wallpaper paste. Shred the paper and leave it in a weak solution of wallpaper paste until it is well-soaked. Press it into the cracks with a filling knife and level it off while still wet.

For wider gaps, cut narrow fillets of wood to fit. Glue each side then hammer them in place; allow them to stand proud of the boards then plane level.

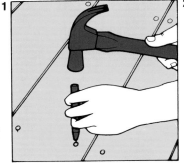
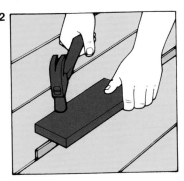

1 Punching nail heads well below the surface of the boards as any left protruding will tear the abrasive sheet on the machine.
2 Filling gaps between boards with fillets of wood glued and hammered into place; plane flush with the boards before sanding.
3 Starting the sander with the drum held above the level of the floor by tilting the machine backwards onto its wheels.

4 Making the first pass, diagonally to the boards; continue parallel to the first pass until most of the floor has been covered.
5 Sanding across the ends of the boards; allow the machine to pull you forwards then drag it backwards for a second pass.
6 Using a scraper or shavehook to scrape stubborn areas at the edges; any low areas which the machine has missed must be sanded by hand.

Stripping old varnish In some older properties, where carpets were used, the boards around the edge of the room were often coated with a varnish stain. This clogs the sanding disk and must be chemically stripped first.

The sander can cope with the stain left by such coatings, so all traces do not have to be removed, just the thick gummy surface.

Sanding the floor

Sanding machines can be rented from tool stores. A drum sander is used for the main area of the floor, a heavy-duty disc sander for the edges. The rental company will supply different grades of abrasive sheets – coarse, medium and fine – and charge for them as used.

As the rented equipment costs money, do all the preparatory work in advance so that the machines can go straight into use and be returned as soon as possible. To speed the operation, one person should sand the main floor area, the other the edges. As well as the sanding equipment a dry hook scraper is useful to get right up to the base board beneath radiators and into corners where the disc sander cannot go.

Protecting the house

Most of the dust is collected into the bags on the sanding machines but a large amount still manages to coat every surface in the room. Protective gauze facemasks can be bought and are well worth while. If it is possible to seal the door with masking tape while doing the sanding to protect the rest of the house, do so. Open the window and have a vacuum cleaner handy to periodically suck up the dust.

Drum sander

Start with the roughest grade abrasive paper – it is commonly held around the drum by a screw-down clamping bar – and sand diagonally across the floor. To start, drape the cable over your shoulder to prevent it from becoming entangled in the machine, and tilt the sander so that the drum is raised. Switch on: do not be alarmed at the great noise caused by the whirring drum – it is quite normal!

Slowly lower the drum onto the floor and in the same movement, allow the machine to roll across the room. Keep the machine on the move for even sanding, and always turn it off when stationary, otherwise you will gorge a deep indent in the floor.

Sand again diagonally from the opposite direction, then follow the grain of the wood, running parallel to the boards. Repeat for the medium-grade paper and finish with the finest-grade. The amount of sanding necessary depends on the floor: two sandings may be sufficient on newer boards.

Disc sander

To use the disc sander, fit an abrasive disc – usually secured with a central bolt – and grasp the two top handles. Stand with legs apart with the sander between and forward. Switch on and run the sander

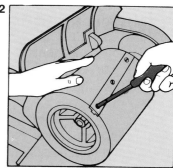

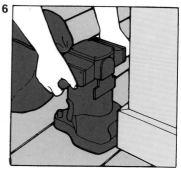

1 Fitting a sheet of coarse abrasive paper to the drum; ensure that it is taut on the drum before screwing down the clamping bar.
2 Tightening the clamping bar screws; make sure that they are fully home otherwise they will cause extensive damage to the floor surface.
3 Making the second pass at right-angles to the first one; the sanding will flatten out any warped or twisted boards.

4 Making the final pass parallel to the boards; repeat the process with medium and fine grades of abrasive, depending on the surface.
5 Changing the abrasive disc; unplug the machine, turn it upside down and remove the locknut and washer, replace in reverse order.
6 Using a heavy-duty disc sander to level areas which are inaccessible to the drum sander; again use decreasingly coarse abrasives.

along the edges. It is not easy to get a smooth finish with a sanding disc attachment to an electric drill.

After sanding, allow at least 24 hours for the dust to settle; the air will be heavy with it. Vacuum the room clean; do not sweep it as this will simply raise the dust. Wash down any ledges, door frames and other obstructions so that dust will not fall on to the floor before the sealant has dried.

VARNISHING WOOD

If wood is not painted, it must be protected with another form of sealant. The easiest sealant to apply is a ready-mixed polyurethane varnish and this is commonly used on floors that have been sanded.

Types of varnish

That most commonly found in hardware stores is the ready to use, polyurethane varnish. It comes in three finishes: flat, mid-sheen (satincoat) and high gloss. Each is as tough as the other. They are all resistant to stains, heat and scratches, and equally easy to apply.

Application

According to the surface being varnished, use a brush or lambswool roller. The varnish should always be applied soon after sanding so that new dirt does not become ingrained. Remember that it is much easier to clean brushes with white spirit than it is rollers.

When varnishing a floor, work from the far corners back towards the door and do not wear shoes.

Dilute the first coat with mineral spirit in the ratio 3 parts varnish: 1 part white spirit. Apply this coat with a cloth pad. It will dry quickly, sealing the wood, and the following coat can be applied within hours.

Brush or roll the varnish on across the grain and then smooth out with the grain (if using a roller, fit a handle extension so you can work by standing). Allow at least six hours between unthinned coats. Ideally, each application should be sanded before the next is applied but this quality of finish is not necessary on a floor. Use at least three coats on a floor, preferably five for a really tough, resistant finish.

Plastic coating can be used on all interior woodwork, including furniture and floors. It is a particularly tough finish, reinforced with melamine. Like plain polyurethane varnish it is clear, has no color and comes in the three finishes, flat, satin and gloss.

Once mixed it stays workable for two to three days. It is extremely quick drying and is touch-dry within the hour. Brush on, following the grain of the wood and leave to harden to a heat-resistant finish that will not chip or crack.

1 Applying a sealing coat of thinned varnish on a clean rag along the grain; work backwards towards the door.
2 When the sealing coat has dried, keying the surface by rubbing lightly with medium sandpaper.
3 Applying the second coat with a brush, working across the grain, after cleaning off all dust with a tack rag.
4 Brushing out the second coat along the grain; use light strokes of the brush and avoid over-spreading.
5 Using a lambswool roller with an extension handle to coat a large floor, working backwards towards the door.

FLOOR COVERINGS

More often than not floor coverings constitute the greatest expense in the decoration of a home. Unlike paint, which can be changed at the touch of a brush, they are expected to give both lasting pleasure and good durability for a number of years.

Although a single covering continuing throughout a house, especially fitted carpet in one color, looks impressive, most householders will take one room at a time. A combination of textures – carpet, wood, hard tile, soft tile – and colors can look pleasing. However, the sub-floor, solid or wooden, may also make different floor coverings more suitable.

Carpet tiles, sheet vinyl or cork could be a choice where carpet is impractical but softness is still a virtue – the kitchen for example. Thermoplastic tiles and uncushioned vinyl – which do not have the same "give" – are better reserved for hallways and other thorough-fares.

Fitted carpet is the obvious choice for bedrooms; although a cheap, light-wear carpet will soon show up the track that develops around the bed.

Children's bedrooms, in particular, should be viewed rather as living rooms when it comes to choosing a carpet and considerable attention given to its wearability. There are ranges designed especially for kitchens and bathrooms where water spillage, cleanliness and condensation are particular problems.

If there is any question of a surface being damp, the choice of floorcovering will be restricted. Thermoplastic vinyl tiles (check the manufacturer's instructions) and quarry tiles can be used here.

Carpet

The classification of carpets is vast and fraught with confusion for the would-be-purchaser, but basically they can be categorized as "woven" or "tufted". Woven types, notably dense-pile Wiltons and multi-hued Axminsters, are made by weaving the pile with a jute or hessian backing; tufted types comprise continuous strands "needled" into a ready-woven backing and secured with adhesive – a foam backing may be stuck to the main backing, obviating the need for a separate underlay.

"Bonded" carpets describe another method of production, in which synthetic fibers are bonded to an impregnated woven backing with adhesive: carpets are made face-to-face then sliced down the middle to make two carpets.

Although you should always aim to buy the very best you can afford, pile length and its treatment are

A selection of floor tiles with soft, hard, warm and cold finishes to suit any situation.

important considerations when buying. There are two main types:
- Looped pile, made by leaving the continuous strands long and uncut, giving textures that are either firm, short twists or knobbly, thick ribs.
- Cut pile, made by cutting the tops off the loops; the pile may be short and stubbly or long and silky (shag). Fiber content is another factor to consider: although the best types are made from wool, they are costly and carpets containing a percentage of man-made fibers are a cheaper alternative, which does not compromise quality. Wholly synthetic-fiber carpets need not be cheap interior substitutes: modern production methods offer wool-lookalikes with the benefit of stain resistance and durability. Typical fibers include hard-wearing nylon; soft, polyester; tough polypropylene (good for "cord" effects) and wool-like acrylic.

Carpets are usually sold in various widths from about 3ft to 16 ½ft. "Broadloom" describes carpets of 6ft width and more; "Body" refers to carpets usually 27 to 35in wide and intended for halls and stairs (although some can be seamed to cover larger areas). "Carpet squares" (not tiles) are large rectangles with bound and finished edges, which are intended as loose-laid rugs.

To avoid excessive wastage, take a plan of the room with its measurements to the supplier. He will work out the most economic method of fitting the carpet and advise on different ranges accordingly. Woven-backed carpets require an underlay (felt or rubber); carpets with built-in foam backing are laid over a lining paper to stop them sticking to the floor.

Carpet tiles

Soft and warm underfoot, carpet tiles score over roll carpet in many ways: because they are loose-laid they can be lifted and rearranged to distribute wear and have the advantage that you can wash them under the faucet; damaged tiles can be replaced with a spare; by mixing colors, checkerboard effects can be created.

Loop and twisted piles are available in tile format in wool or natural fiber and should have a thick rubber backing. Sizes are typically 16in square.

Sheet vinyl

Soft and warm underfoot, sheet vinyl is unbeatable for ease of cleaning and durability in areas of heavy wear. It is available in 6ft 6in, 9ft 9in and 13ft widths, making it ideal for covering an average-sized room without the need for seams. Most vinyl sheet is laid loose; where joins are unavoidable the seams can be stuck down with special adhesive.
● Unbacked vinyl. This is made from a PVC backing printed with a pattern then protected by a thin transparent PVC layer. Solid vinyl has the color running through the whole thickness of the material.
● Backed vinyl. This has a backing layer or "cushion" of foamed PVC (sometimes felt).

Many sheet vinyls have an embossed pattern, frequently imitating a tiled or brick effect.

Vinyl tiles

These are extremely tough and hardwearing and typically measure between 8 to 12in sq.
● Cushioned vinyl tiles. Exactly like sheet vinyl but could save on wastage in a small or awkwardly shaped room. They are soft, warm underfoot and easy to clean. They are sold in packs and are self-adhesive.
● Plain vinyl tiles. Very resilient but colder and harder underfoot than the cushioned ones. They are an obvious choice for hallways and other areas where resilience is more important than comfort. They also come in packs; some are self-adhesive.
● Thermoplastic tiles. Tough, expensive and applied with adhesive – may be suitable for use where there is the slight possibility of damp.

Cork tiles

Polyurethane-sealed or unsealed, both with a pleasing natural appearance created by compressed cork granules glued together then sawn to produce tiles typically 12in sq (seal unsealed varieties after laying). Cork tiles are good insulators and an excellent choice for bathrooms, where they are warm under-foot. Non-adhesive and self adhesive tiles are available.

Ceramic tiles

Available in a range of colors, smoothly glazed ceramic floor tiles differ from their wall-hung counterparts in that they are thicker due to the wear they are likely to receive – typically ⅜in. They are ideal for use in kitchens and bathrooms. Frost-resistant versions are also available for outside paths and patios.

Although square tiles are most popular, (measuring from about 4in sq) there are rectangular units of these squares, octagons, hexagons and interlocking styles.

Most tiles are square-edged and unglazed but some may have two glazed edges for use as steps. Some tiles are made with spacer lugs attached but plastic spacers can be used instead.

Quarry tiles

Quarry tiles are unglazed ceramic tiles that are particularly useful where the floor is subject to heavy wear; they can also be used outdoors as a surface for a patio. They come in various sizes – commonly 3, 6 and 9in sq – and thicknesses of ½, ⅝ or 1 ¼in and in subtle browns, reds and yellows. There are also rectangles and octagons and specially-cut tiles available. They have to be laid in a bed of sand/cement mortar which is smoothed out between battens and when dry, grouted like ceramic tiles.

Mosaic and wood block flooring

Parquet tiles – or mosaic floor panels – are 5⁄16in thick "fingers" of wood stuck to a bituminous felt backing or wired together to form a square: the squares are arranged as 12in or 18in sq panels in basketweave design and are usually glued to a suitable subfloor.

Traditional wood blocks, usually about 10in long and 2¾in wide by ¾in thick, are laid in basketweave, herringbone or stretcher bonds to create a tough, resilient surface. Some blocks are tongued and grooved and can be slotted together. They are normally bedded in hot pitch, although special flooring adhesive can be used.

Wood strip flooring

Strip flooring is made up from separate strips of solid or laminated hardwood. They measure between about 16in and 6ft long, between 2¾ and 8in wide and ⅜, ¾ or ⅞in thick (solid) or ¼ to ¾in thick (laminated). Strips are usually tongued-and-grooved for slotting together; some strips also come in tile form, resembling long wood planks when laid.

Laminated strips are made pre-finished, as are some solid versions, although the latter must usually be sanded and sealed after laying.

LAYING A CARPET

The average householder is not likely to spend hundreds of dollars on a new carpet, then save comparatively few by fitting it himself: mistakes can happen, and you would have no one to blame but yourself if you ruined the floorcovering. Knowing how to fit a carpet does come in useful, for example, when you have moved house and you have old but perfectly good carpets to be re-used, or perhaps you would risk laying a cheaper quality carpet yourself. The carpet must, of course, be larger than the room for which it is intended. It may be entirely the wrong shape and necessitate a lot of trimming. Lay it down in the room and trim it down to 3in larger than needed all round. This will make fitting more manageable.

When making joins, the pile must always face the same way. If a strip is cut from the length and turned at 90 degrees to make up the width, the change in the direction of pile will show. This may be acceptable where, for example, an alcove is to be filled or most of the strip will be hidden by furniture.

The carpet should be arranged so that the pile faces towards the door and away from the main source of light. If a join must be made, try to avoid the area of heaviest traffic and always make the join along the traffic area rather than across it. Where a join is used to make up the width of a room, it should be on the side away from the door. Do not attempt to lay carpet on an uneven floor: the edges of boards will soon rub away at the underlay or woven backing and will create lines in the carpet. Nail down loose boards, turn warped ones or plane down the edges against the grain and fill any large cracks.

Solid floors with a mortar screed can be carpeted but there must be a waterproof membrane and the surface must be absolutely dry and smooth.

Foam-backed carpet

This is much easier to lay than the woven variety: it needs no underlay, no stretching and no gripper rods or tacks. It is stuck to the floor around the perimeter of the room with double-sided tape. To prevent the foam backing sticking to the floorboards under friction, and tearing away when the carpet is lifted, a paper lining is arranged over the boards. Special paper can be bought or use strong brown paper.

Firstly, cover the floor to within 2in of the wall with the paper underlay. Join it if necessary with single-sided adhesive tape and fix it around the edges with double-sided tape. Stick lengths of double-sided adhesive tape all around the room.

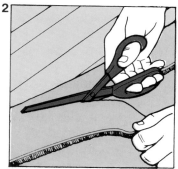
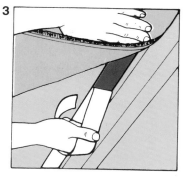
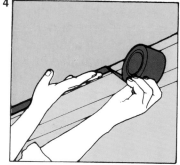

1 Laying foam-backed carpet: After fixing the threshold strip, unrolling the carpet with the pile sloping away from the window.
2 After stretching the carpet and creasing into the floor/baseboard angle; cut along the crease for an exact fit.

3 With the carpet trimmed to lap up the walls 3in, sticking double-sided tape to the floor alongside the paper-felt underlay.
4 Peeling off the backing strip of the double-sided tape before pressing the carpet onto it; keep the carpet taut as you proceed.

Spread out the carpet on the floor so that it laps up the base all round. Roughly trim off the excess with a sharp trimming knife – cut through the foam backing not the pile side – leaving about 3in all round.

At chimney breast alcoves, push the carpet up against the face of the protrusion, the excess folded back on itself. Measure off the depth of alcove then make a cut this length parallel with the side of the chimney breast – allow 3in for trimming. Cut off the end of the piece that fits into the alcove, again allowing a margin for trimming, then cut along the face of the chimney breast.

To fit the carpet into a corner, grasp the overlap and push your thumb deep into the baseboard angle. Pull away the carpet with your thumb still in place and cut off the corner of carpet just beyond it.

Trim the edges of the carpet all round, by pressing the overlaps well into the baseboard angle with a paint scraper or flat chisel. Pull back the carpet and trim along the score mark.

Peel the backing off the double-sided tape, and smooth the carpet down on to it.

Woven carpet

There are two ways to lay woven carpet: by tacking or with tackless fittings. Whichever you choose an underlay is needed. A knee-kicker, which can be rented, is used for stretching the carpet into place.

Tackless fittings give a better finish as no tacks are used through the face of the carpet. The fittings, or gripper strips, are thin wood laths with barbs, which are nailed in a continuous line around the room with a gap between them and the wall slightly less than the uncompressed thickness of the carpet. Punch down the nail heads. Cut the strips to length using pruning shears or use a sharp knife. Arrange short lengths to fit around obstructions.

Before laying the underlay, it is very important to make sure the floor is clean and free from any form of debris that may become trapped underneath and show up as raised bumps. Position the underlay right up to the inside edge of the gripper rods and tack it, staple it, or stick it to the floor with double-sided tape. Join any seams with adhesive carpet tape (plus a latex adhesive if the underlay is felt).

The carpet has to be stretched over the gripper rods to be held firm and flat by the barbs. Roll it out in the room, leaving the surplus riding up the walls all round. Trim off the surplus, leaving about 2in overlap. Use the knee-kicker to stretch the carpet taut over the barbs on the gripper rods: set the tool's pins to the correct depth, press the head into the carpet pile to pierce the weave then nudge the padded end with your knee to stretch the carpet.

"Kick" the carpet to one of the adjoining corners and again, hook it into position. Work back along the wall to the first corner, stretching the carpet onto the gripper with the knee-kicker, leaving the surplus sticking up all along.

Work from the first corner to the other adjoining corner and back along this wall. Repeat from this corner to the final corner, stretching the carpet across the room and hooking it onto the strips. Trim down the surplus to about 3/8in and turn this down into the gap between the strips and the wall. Use a flat bolster chisel to push the cut edge into the gap. Leave the surplus at the doorway to be fitted into a special edging strip or binder bar.

1 Laying woven-backed carpet: Nailing gripper strip one carpet-thickness away from the baseboard; protect with a piece of card.
2 Laying the foam-rubber underlay; butt one end of the first length up to the gripper strip and cut to fit. Repeat the process at the other end.
3 Using a knee kicker to stretch the carpet onto the grippers; adjust the teeth to grip the woven backing, press down and knee-kick the pad.
4 After fixing all around the room, trimming the edges of the carpet with a sharp knife to leave 3/8in lapping up the baseboard.
5 With the carpet held taut with the knee kicker, push the surplus into the gap behind the gripper strips with a bolster chisel.
6 Cutting to fit around a hearth; fold back the carpet over a piece of board and cut to a loose fit through the backing.
7 Fitting to an internal corner; press the thumb firmly into the angle, grip the carpet and lift it away from the corner.
8 Making a cut just beyond the tip of the thumb before cutting diagonally across the corner of the carpet and pressing back into position.

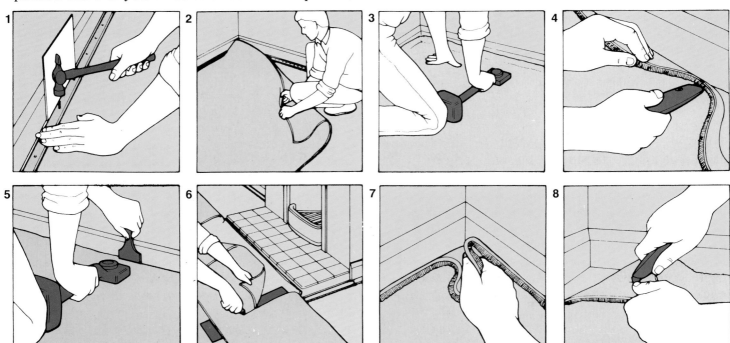

Seams and doorways

Foam-backed carpet is easily joined with adhesive carpet tape. Fit it to one edge and roll the other on to it, butting the two edges neatly.

Woven-backed carpets are joined with latex glue and carpet seaming tape. Brush the adhesive up the pile to prevent fraying.

At doorways, carpet should extend under the center of the closed door: there are aluminum edging strips for both foam-backed and woven carpets. Where two carpets meet in a doorway, use a special strip which incorporates two barbed flanges and a common edge strip. Screw the bar into position (use glue on a concrete floor), stretch the carpet into place, trim and hook over the barbs. Where the carpet meets a smooth floor-covering, use an edging strip that incorporates barbs one side for the carpet and a retaining flange for the vinyl (or whatever is used).

Joining woven-backed carpet; brush latex glue onto the backing, the edge of the pile and the tape. Allow to dry and then press together.

At a doorway, using a bolster chisel to push the edge of the carpet under the center bar of the threshold strip.

Fitting around pipes

You will probably have to cut the carpet to fit around central heating and plumbing pipes emerging from the floor. To do this, fit the carpet up to the wall on which the pipe is located then make an incision in the edge parallel with the center of the pipe; measure from the baseboard to the pipe then cut out a small circle of carpet this distance from its edge.

To neaten the cut edge around the pipe, you may prefer to turn under a small amount of the carpet and stick down using a thin coating of fabric adhesive.

LAYING STAIR CARPET

Stairs can be carpeted with fitted carpet or what is called a runner, narrower strip carpeting. This is the easier of the two methods. A woven carpet runner also allows the carpet to be moved from time to time to equalize wear. Old-fashioned stair rods with side clips can be used to hold a runner in place and form part of the stair decor, but it is now more usual to use gripper strips. Special pinless grippers are available for use with foam-backed carpets: the carpet is held in tight jaws. The wooden strips are used in pairs, one at the back of the tread, one at the bottom of the riser, or you can buy a metal version that is already formed into a right angle.

Cut the strips to length, if necessary, 1½in shorter than the width of the carpet using tinsnips or secateurs for the wooden strips, a hacksaw for the metal type. Nail them into place, omitting the bottom riser. The gap between each pair of wooden strips should be just big enough to squeeze the carpet down into it. Cut the underlay to fit between the rods and tack close to the rods, omitting the bottom tread. No underlay is needed with foam-backed carpet.

Fitting a woven carpet
With a runner, an extra length of carpet is included so that it can be moved up to even out the wear taken on the treads; this is folded underneath the bottom step. The pile should run down the stairs to prevent uneven shading and promote longer wear.

Start at the bottom of the stairs. Tack the end of the carpet face downwards to the bottom tread, at the back, close to the gripper. Run it down over the tread to the bottom of the last riser, fold it back and tack the fold to the riser and tread. Run the carpet up the stairs, stretching it over the gripper rods and pushing it down between them with a flat chisel. It should join any landing carpet at the top of the last riser. If there is no carpet on the landing take the stair runner over the top of the final riser, turn under the edge and tack down.

Fitting on winding stairs
Where the stairs go round a bend, gripper rods cannot be used in the usual way. The carpet need not be cut but can be folded to fit the turn.
Woven carpet Fit the gripper rods only to the treads on winding stairs. Fold the surplus carpet, with the fold falling downwards, and tack it to the bottom of the riser at 3in intervals. Working upwards, repeat the stretching, folding and tacking process.

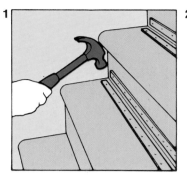

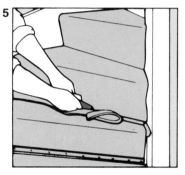

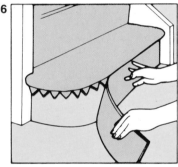

1 Tacking gripper strips to the back of the tread and the bottom of the riser, leaving a gap into which the carpet can be pushed.
2 Fixing underlay to the treads and risers with a staple gun to butt up to the gripper strips; continue the landing underlay to the top riser.
3 Tacking down carpet on an open landing; fold under the edge and tack through both thicknesses by each baluster.
4 Working from the top downwards, stretching the carpet and pushing it between the gripper strips with a bolster chisel; take care not to cut it.

5 Cutting off surplus carpet on a winder; cover each tread separately, cutting off along the crease at the gripper strips.
6 After tacking through zig-zag flaps turned under a bullnose tread, fitting a covering strip; tack through the top edge and both ends.

Foam-backed Omit the pinless rods altogether on winding stairs. Tack the carpet to the tread, right at the back so that the tacks are not too noticeable. Fold down the surplus and tack to the bottom of the riser.

Fitting stair carpet

The fixings for a fitted stair carpet are as for a runner. The extra length of woven carpet is not needed at the bottom, and underlay should be fitted to all the steps. The gripper rods should be the full width of the stairs. Fit the carpet from the top of the flight. The landing carpet should overlap on to the stairs and down to the bottom of the uppermost riser. The stair carpet must be stretched over the gripper rods as usual, pushed down between them; and trimmed to fit at the edges. No fixings are needed at the edges.

Winding stairs

The treatment on winding stairs will depend partially on the type of carpet. However, whatever the carpet, a simple fold on the riser will not do. Each tread and the riser below it must be fitted individually, the carpet cut to size each time.

With a woven carpet, fit rods to both the treads and risers as on a straight run and also along the outside edge of the tread. Cut the carpet to fit over the rod at the back of the tread and down onto the rod at the bottom of the riser below. Cut and fit the underlay to lie in between the rods. Stretch the carpet over, trimming it at the edges and pulling it over the rod at the outside edge. Repeat on each winding stair.

With a foam-backed carpet, gripper rods cannot be used. The carpet must be cut to fit each tread and the riser below, allowing a turn-under at the bottom. The pieces are tacked into place. Fit the lowest piece first, turning under the bottom edge, tacking it to the riser, pulling it up over the tread and tacking it flat right at the back of the tread. The next piece, its end tucked under and tacked to the riser, will conceal the tacks on the tread below, giving a neater finish. The side edges need not be turned under or fixed.

Pushing foam-backed carpet between tackless grippers with a bolster chisel.

LAYING SHEET VINYL

Sheet vinyl is the successor to linoleum, but combines the virtues of linoleum and carpet. It is extremely durable and completely waterproof but is also soft and warm underfoot. An advantage with sheet vinyl is that being available in three widths: 6ft 6in, 9ft 9in and 13ft, it is usually possible to cover a floor without any joins.

Preparation

Sheet vinyl can be laid on both wooden and solid floors, provided that they are both absolutely smooth and the solid floor has a waterproof membrane. Check the condition of the air-vents under a wooden floor and if necessary, increase the number to ensure efficient underfloor ventilation.

The roll of vinyl should be left in the room in which it is to be used (lying down, not stored on end) for at least 24 hours before any fitting commences so that it will acclimatize.

Fitting and trimming

Unroll the vinyl and cut it roughly to fit, leaving about an extra 2 or 3in all round. If any joins are to be made and a pattern matched, take this into account when bringing the two sheets roughly to size.

It is unlikely that any one wall will be perfectly straight, but if one looks straight, butt the edge of the vinyl up to it. Stand in the door way and assess the appearance. If the pattern looks straight and central on the floor then work from this straight edge. If it does not look absolutely right, it is better to trim this edge as well.

Pull the vinyl away from the wall by about 1in, keeping the vinyl straight to the room as a whole, not the wall. Use either a pair of compasses or a short block of wood and a felt-tipped pen to mark a line on the vinyl exactly following the line on the wall.

Run one leg of the compass along the baseboard, the pen on the vinyl, or move the block of wood along the baseboard, holding the pen close against the other side all the time.

Cut along this line with a sharp trimming knife and push the vinyl into place against the baseboard. It will be a perfect fit, overlapping at each end on to the adjoining walls.

To trim the next straight edge, use a block of wood to push the vinyl into the angle between the floor and baseboard. Then, either cut along the crease with a trimming knife freehand or mark the line in pen, and cut along the line.

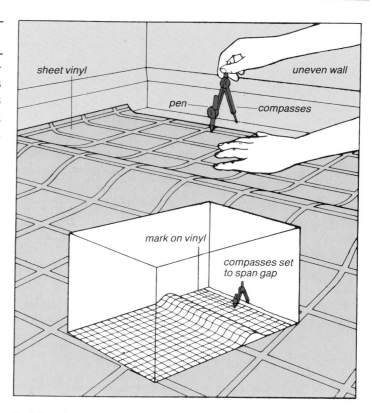

Scribing along an uneven wall; mark where one end of the sheet meets the wall and pull the sheet back squarely until the end lies flat. Set the compasses to span the gap between the wall and the mark, and run the point of the compasses along the angle with the pen on the vinyl.

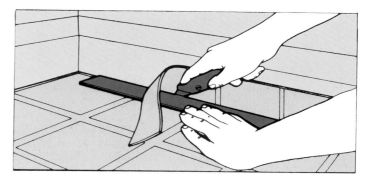

Trimming along a straight wall; push the end of the sheet firmly into the wall angle with a metal straight-edge, making sure that the rest of the sheet is lying flat, and cut along between the straight-edge and the wall with a sharp knife to remove the surplus.

Joining sheets of vinyl

If two sheets are to be joined, cut both roughly to size. In doing this allow extra on the length in order to match the pattern. The tile designs on sheet vinyl are arranged so that the sheets can be butted together and the pattern becomes continuous, as in the case of matching wallpaper.

Having fitted one sheet, overlap and move the second sheet along to match the pattern exactly. Trim to fit as with the first sheet. The join is then made by cutting through both sheets of vinyl, through the mid-point of the overlap using your straight edge and sharp cutting knife.

All joins should be firmly secured (see Adhesives on page 51).

Fitting around obstructions

At an internal corner where surplus vinyl runs up both walls, trim away the corner of the vinyl bit by bit until it can lie flat on the floor. The two straight edges can then be trimmed in the usual way.

At an external corner, cut down through the vinyl following the line of the protruding corner. It may be necessary to cut a narrow V-shape if the line is not straight. The two straight edges can then be pressed against the baseboard and trimmed in the usual way.

At door frames or other obstructions, make vertical cuts down through the surplus vinyl, keeping the blade of the trimming knife close to the contour of the obstruction. Trim away the surplus by joining the vertical cuts with horizontal ones.

Making a template

In a small bathroom where the obstructions are awkwardly shaped, see opposite page, it will be simpler all round to make paper templates for cutting the vinyl to fit exactly. Fit the vinyl roughly to the walls first, making incisions inwards from the edge where it meets a basin pedestal or toilet base, so that it will lie almost flat.

Take a sheet of stiff paper that is about 1in larger than the obstacle and gently tear it to fit roughly around half the base. Fit another sheet at the other side of the obstacle. Use a pencil and a block of wood to scribe the profile of the obstacle on the template.

Lay the template on top of the vinyl and secure it with adhesive tape. Transfer the profile to the vinyl by first running the pencil and block along the scribed line. Working freehand, cut the vinyl to shape then fit it around the obstacle first making a straight cut at the back, (in the case of a pedestal) and joining the edges when fitting.

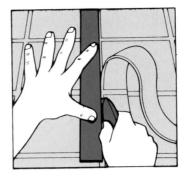
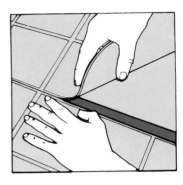

Joining lengths of vinyl by overlapping the two sheets until the pattern matches and cutting through both thicknesses.

Joining the cut edges with double-sided tape; after removing the offcuts, butt join the edges along the tape and press down firmly.

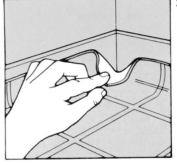

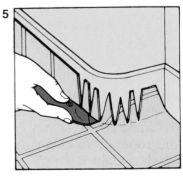

1 Fitting sheet vinyl to an internal corner: With the sheet flat on the floor, bending back the surplus to form a crease mark in the corner.
2 After pulling back the sheet from the corner, cutting diagonally through the crease; push into the corner and trim along the walls.
3 With a straight-edge along one side of an external corner and across the vinyl, cutting along it before sliding the sheet into the corner.
4 Fitting at doorways: Leave a flap overlapping the threshold and make a series of vertical cuts down the contours of the architrave.

5 At a curved corner, making a series of vertical release cuts to allow the vinyl to lie flat before trimming around the curve.

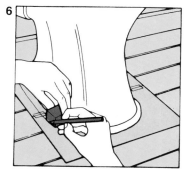

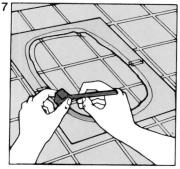

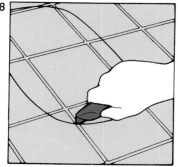

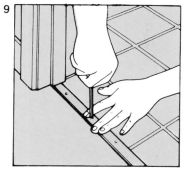

6 Fitting around a pedestal: Making a paper template by tearing two halves to a rough fit, taping together and scribing around against a block.
7 After sticking the template in the correct position on the vinyl, scribing onto the vinyl by running the block inside the line.

8 Trimming around the marked contour; to fit the vinyl around the pedestal, make a straight cut to the edge and join the edges after fitting.
9 Fitting a threshold strip in a doorway to secure the ege and prevent tripping; choose a type to suit the adjoining floorcovering.

Adhesives

Check the manufacturer's instructions for the recommended method of fixing the vinyl. Some can be laid loose, and others can be secured with a double-sided tape or liquid adhesive.

The double-sided tape can be stuck to the floor prior to fitting the vinyl, leaving the backing on. When the vinyl has been trimmed to size, remove the backing and press the vinyl onto the sticky band. On large areas remove only short lengths of backing and tape on the vinyl, repeating this until the floor is completely covered.

Liquid adhesive can be applied in a strip all around the room or to cover the entire floor. Roll back the vinyl, weight it lightly and apply a band of adhesive about 4in wide with a notched spreader. Release the vinyl on to it and press down.

Secure joins between the sheets in the same way, but spread the adhesive in a band 8in wide. Press the edges of the vinyl together over the adhesive, using a broom to work along the seam.

If the whole floor area is to be covered with adhesive, do half at a time: roll back the vinyl, spread the adhesive and release the vinyl on to it. Treat the other side of the floor in exactly the same way. Use a broom to flatten down the vinyl and to squeeze out any trapped air bubbles.

Edging strips

As with carpets, a neat edge is achieved at a doorway with a binder bar. Buy one to suit the thickness of the vinyl, cut to length if necessary and fit with the screws provided or nails, slotting in the edge of the vinyl under the metal rim.

LAYING CERAMIC FLOOR TILES

Ceramic tiles made for use on the floor are thicker than those designed for walls. They often do not have spacer lugs (the little notches on the edges, which set the tiles the correct width apart for grouting). Should your tiles not have spacer lugs, plastic spacers can be bought – these will be embedded in the base material so they do not have to be removed.

Preparing the floor

The ideal base for ceramic floor tiles is solid concrete. This should be level, dry and free from grit, dirt and grease. If it is uneven it can be leveled with a self-leveling compound. Seal the floor with a diluted coat of PVA adhesive or a primer recommended by the manufacturer of the adhesive to be used.

Marking the square

Ceramic floor tiles should be arranged so that they are square with the doorway rather than a straight wall. This keeps the pattern effect regular, especially in a room that is an odd shape. If the tiles are not square to the door, the effect will be lopsided. First, mark out the area by drawing a line across the doorway, against which the tiles will fit. Find the center point on this line and measure out from it a 90 degree angle into the room. Set a batten to this point and extend it in pencil or chalk across the room to the opposite wall.

Place a tile into the right angle at the center of the door. Allowing a ⅛in gap between tiles for spacers, move the tile up the line, marking where each tile will be. At the opposite wall stop when the mark for the last complete tile has been made. Secure a batten across the floor, its inner edge to this point, making sure it is fixed at right angles to the drawn line from the doorway and regardless of the wall behind it. Fix a second batten at right angles to the first at one end of

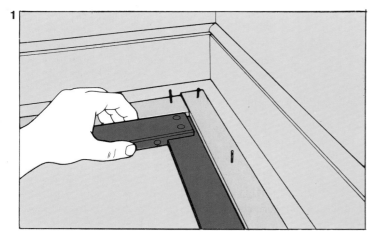

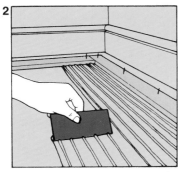

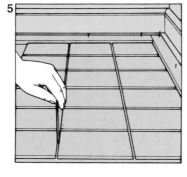

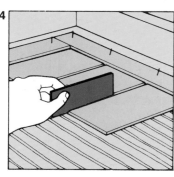

the room. This creates a perfect square in which the first tile can be fixed.

To see how the finished effect will look and where tiles will have to be cut, you can lay out all the tiles dry, starting from this corner.

Remember to allow for spacers between the tiles. If it seems that some awkward cutting will be necessary and can be avoided by moving the side batten a little further into the room or out, do so.

Laying the tiles

The adhesive for all ceramic tiles is applied to the floor or wall, not the tiles. On a solid floor, a cement-based adhesive is usually used; on a wooden floor use the same mixture if the surface is primed, otherwise opt for a cement-rubber type.

Mix the adhesive following the manufacturer's instructions and spread it with a trowel across an area of about one square yard, in the starting corner. Adhesive is usually spread on in a ⅛in thick layer but some "thick bed" types are spread to ½in thickness for uneven floors. Using the grooved spreader provided, draw ridges through the adhesive.

Press the first tile into position with a slight twisting movement; do not slide it into place. This ensures that the entire back of the tile is bedded in the adhesive. Plastic spacers can be bought which fit on the corner of the tiles to hold them the required width apart. Put one on the protruding corner of the tile to make sure the two adjoining tiles are the correct distance apart. The spacer pegs do not have to be removed prior to grouting. Continue fitting tiles and spacers until the adhesive has been covered. Wipe away the excess adhesive from the edges and spread a second square yard ready for tiling. Continue in this way until all the whole tiles are in position, then remove the battens.

Cutting border tiles

Each border tile must be cut individually to fit the space between the whole tiles and the base. To make the cuts you can use either a tungsten carbide-tipped tile scorer or a cutting tool; the easiest to use works like pliers to snap the tile along a scored line. Other, more complex (and costly) devices feature a marking, scoring and cutting jig – this may be worth the investment, or renting, if the room is large and there are a lot of tiles to cut.

To mark the tile for cutting or breaking, hold it face down in place against the wall, over-lapping the tile already stuck down. Allowing for the spacer peg between the two tiles, mark in pencil on each edge,

1 Fitting temporary guide battens for laying ceramic floor tiles; after marking on the floor the position of the last full row of tiles to give equal-width cut tiles at each end, nail the battens to the floor, square to each other, outside the marked lines.
2 Spreading adhesive with a notched spreader over an area of 10sq ft. Ensure the notches are the correct depth for the tiles.

3 Positioning the first tile in the corner of the guide battens; push it tightly against the battens and press down firmly and evenly.
4 Continuing laying tiles along the first row; use a piece of card or spacer pegs to leave equal gaps between the tiles for grouting.
5 Completing the tiling over the first area of adhesive before spreading a further 10sq ft. Check that the tiles are level.

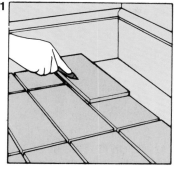

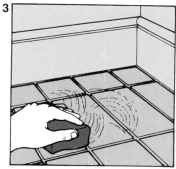

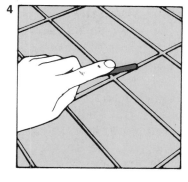

1 Marking the width of edging tiles; postion over the last full tile, and mark against its edge, allowing for grouting.
2 After scoring a straight line across the tile through the mark with the tile cutter, snapping the tile between the jaws.

3 After completing the tiling and allowing the recommended drying time, sponging a slurry of grout into the joints to seal them.
4 Using a pointed piece of wood or a grouting tool to round off the grout in a slight downward curve.

the overlapping amount that must be removed. Turn the tile face up and using a straight edge and a scorer, cut through the glazed surface, joining together the two pencil marks.

Kneel on the floor, grip a spare tile between the knees, hold the tile to be cut with one hand on each side of the score line and bring it down on to the edge of the outer tile. It should break cleanly. If it does not break at all, use one of the stronger tile cutters available. You can even buy a special tile-cutting blade – either a round-section "rod saw" or a flat blade – to fit a hacksaw and this is useful with particularly stubborn tiles or where you have to cut out curves and notches.

Smooth the cut edge with a carborundum stone, rubbing it along the edge not across it. Check the fit, putting the tile in position with the cut edge to the wall. Apply adhesive to the back of the tile and stick it down firmly. Do not forget the spacers.

Where tiles need more than one edge-cut it will be better to use a tile cutter or saw for the job. If the amount is small, use a pair of pincers to nibble off the surplus, bit by bit. Once in position and grouted, the

unevenness will not be noticeable.

To mark up for an external corner and in order to keep the cut edges to the wall, put the tile to be cut face up on top of the adjacent whole one, on one side of the corner. Put a spare tile on top of this, but with its edge to the wall, and mark a line across as though for a straight cut.

Do not turn the tile, but move it to the whole tile adjacent to the other side of the corner and use the spare tile to mark a line across for a straight line at right angles to the first. Cut out the surplus area between the two lines and the remaining bit of tile will fit exactly – cut edge to the wall.

For an internal corner, put the tile to be cut face down on the whole tile central to the corner. Use a spare tile held against the wall to mark the two lines to be cut. When flipped over to face the right way up, the cut edges will be to the wall.

Where a more complicated cut has to be made, such as around a curving architrave, treat as an external corner with the tile to be cut face up on the adjacent whole tile. Use a spare tile to mark the cutting lines and join any curving ones by working freehand. A tile-cutting rod saw is very useful for cutting such intricate lines.

Finishing off
Leave the floor for at least 24 hours for the adhesive to set firm (check the manufacturer's instructions on this point). Do not walk on the floor during this time. Make sure that any surplus adhesive is wiped off while still wet.

Grouting
To finish off, the gaps between each tile are filled with grout. Grouting can be done as soon as the adhesive has set. Mix the grout with clean water to a thick paste. However, it is better not to mix too much at one time as it hardens quite quickly.

Apply the grout with the flat spreader provided, taking it over the tiles and forcing it into the joins. Clean off the spreader and scrape it over the tiles to remove the excess grout. Use your fingertip to press the grout in between the tiles and smooth it. As the grout starts to dry, dampen the sponge and smooth it lightly over the tiles to clean them. Rinse the sponge frequently in clean water. When completely dry, give a wipe all over with a dry cloth.

If the tiles form a lip in the doorway, a piece of angled beading or strip of hardwood will protect the edge. Alternatively, shaped quadrant tiles are available for this purpose.

LAYING SOFT FLOOR TILES

Soft floor tiles include: carpet tiles, cork tiles, vinyl tiles and rubber tiles, see pages 46–47.

There are various methods for laying these tiles: some are self-adhesive, some are laid loose and some are laid on a bed of adhesive. They all, however, require a sound, dry, clean, level surface. Before laying the tiles, all surfaces will need to be thoroughly scoured with steel wool to rid them not only of dirt and grease but also of old polish finishes.

Setting out the floor

Whether the tiles are laid loose or stuck down, the marking out of the floor is the same.

First, find the center point of the floor. Do this by finding the center point on each of the walls, measuring straight along and ignoring bay windows and doors. Take two lengths of string, coat them with chalk and pin them from one wall to the opposite. The two strings will cross in the middle of the floor at right angles to each other denoting the center of the room. Snap each string across the floor to leave a chalk line;

remove the strings but leave the pins for now.

Set out a row of tiles dry from the center point to one wall. Check the size of the border. Continue the line of tiles to the opposite wall to check the width of that border. Move the tiles a little either way to even up the borders – aim for a margin no less than half a tile wide. Move the pins on each wall to measure the same distance.

Do the same with a row of tiles between the other two walls, and adjust them as necessary. Move the pins to compensate.

Remove the dry tiles, refit the strings and chalk two fresh lines. The cross will mark where the first tiles are to be laid.

Loose-laid tiles

Carpet tiles are laid loose. Most have a non-slip back but may require strategic spots of latex adhesive if slipping is a problem.

From the chalked cross, lay a row of tiles across the room from one wall to the opposite one. Butt the tiles together, (see diagram 2). Cut and fit the border pieces (see diagrams 3 and 4), cutting from the back.

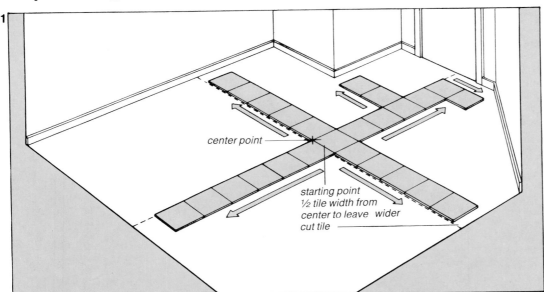

center point

starting point
½ tile width from
center to leave wider
cut tile

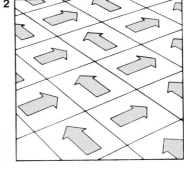

1 When laying floor tiles it is important to dry-lay a few tiles to find out where cut tiles will be and to adjust their widths to give a balanced effect. Starting from the measured center point of the floor (X), work outwards in a cross shape in the direction of the arrows and adjust the starting point as needed.
2 The direction of the pile may be marked on the reverse side with an arrow; lay the pile in alternate directions for a subtle chequerboard effect.
3 Marking border tile; lay over last full tile, lay second tile on top butting up to baseboard and mark along its edge.
4 Marking tile for external corner; follow procedure for straight border tile but repeat on second face of corner.

Laying quarry tiles

Quarry tiles are unglazed ceramic tiles. Like glazed ceramic tiles they are tough and easy to clean. They can be laid with flooring adhesive or bedded in mortar.

Quarry tiles are difficult to cut so plan a simple layout, avoiding awkward cutting and very narrow spaces. Calculate the quantity needed by multiplying the length and width of the area and dividing by the size of the tile. Round up the number and allow an extra five per cent for breakages.

Clean sound concrete thoroughly. Stabilize powdery concrete with a priming coat of PVA adhesive. For a wooden floor to be suitable there must be no movement in it, loose boards must be nailed securely and the surface leveled with plywood. Loose-laid floorcovering must be lifted but existing fixed tiles can be left in place.

To fix tiles it is necessary to create a bay into which the mortar is spread; you can then arrange the tiles on top. When one bay is completed, the battens are removed and set up again alongside. Starting on a straight wall in one corner, (preferably away from a door) fix two battens – they should be twice as thick as the tiles – at right angles to each other. Make a tiling gauge to plot the positions of the tiles on the floor: plot four tile-widths away along the wall and fix a third batten in this position at right-angles. Check that the battens are horizontal with a spirit level and pack them up with cardboard.

Fill the bay with a fairly crumbly mortar mix (3 parts sand: 1 part cement) and level off by dragging across it a board cut to span the battens and notched at each end the thickness of a tile. As you draw the board along the sides of the bay, the lower edge, recessed between the battens, will level off the mortar to the correct depth. Use the tiling gauge to position the tiles on the mortar. When the 16 tiles are in place, tap them down into the mortar with a block of wood. Check their evenness with a spirit level. Lift the third batten and reposition it to form another bay – four tiles wide – next to the tiles already laid.

As a section is finished the edging tiles can be cut to fit. Score deeply along the cutting line with a tile cutter. Tap with a pin hammer on the underside of the tile on the scoring line to break the tile. Bite away small pieces at a time using pincers.

Fix the base by buttering the back of each tile with mortar. Press into place, lining the tiles up with those already positioned on the floor.

Grout the tiles after 24 hours with a flooring grout, rubbing it in well.

Drawing a leveling batten across the crumbly 3:1 mortar; notch the ends to the depth of one tile thickness.

Tamping the tiles level in the first bay with a block of wood; check in all directions with a level.

After moving one side batten four tile-widths along, leveling the second bed across the batten and the laid tiles.

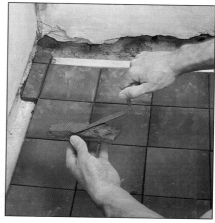

Buttering the back of a cut tile with mortar to fill in the gaps around the edges left after removing the battens.

Pressing the cut tiles into position; then refix the original baseboard or fix quarry tile base in the same way.

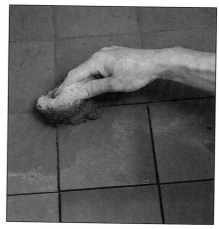

After 24 hours, grouting with flooring grout mixed to a creamy consistency; rub well into the gaps with a sponge.

WOOD-BLOCK/WOOD-STRIP FLOORING

Wood-block flooring is also available in easy-to-lay tiles as an alternative to the individual blocks. The pieces come in a variety of sizes and in a pattern; either tongued-and-grooved or bonded to a paper backing, ready to be stuck to the floor with the recommended adhesive. Parquet tiles, as they are known, come ready-sanded and some ready-sealed.

An acrylic seal makes the tiles particularly hard-wearing. The sanded ones can be finished with several coats of polyurethane varnish. They can be stuck to both solid and wooden floors provided they are firm, level and dry without special preparation.

Wood-strip flooring comes in long strips, which are tongued-and-grooved to slot together. Some come with fixing clips which are driven into the adjacent boards; others are secret-nailed through the tongue so that the nails do not show on the surface and yet others are fixed with adhesive. The strips can be used on solid and wooden floors and in a thicker form.

Uneven wooden floors will have to be leveled with hardboard and uneven solid floors with a self-leveling compound. Do not use where there is damp.

Laying parquet tiles
Set out the floor as for soft floor tiles. Loose-lay some tiles and adjust the fit as necessary. Spread the adhesive on the floor and begin when it is tacky. At the sides of the room leave an expansion gap of ⅜in. Use cork strip or a quarter round beading nailed to the base (not the floor) to conceal the gap. To trim tiles, cut through the backing between the strips. Cut intricate shapes with a saw, using a template for accurate measurement.

Laying wood-strip flooring
Some manufacturers recommend laying plastic under the boards while others provide a special underlay.

The base can be removed or not; if it is, when it is replaced, it will cover the expansion gap that must be left at the sides of the room. Door frames will need trimming at the bottom.

Begin laying the strip flooring parallel to the longest wall bearing in mind that on wood floors the strips must run the opposite way to the floor boards. Lay complete rows with the tongue out on tongued-and-grooved boards.

Chalk a straight line across the room from the door and another at right angles to this. This forms a set square for the room on which further guidelines can be drawn. To determine the expansion gap, fit

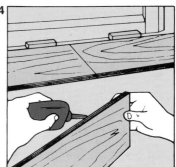
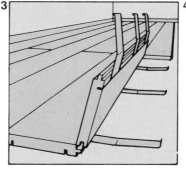

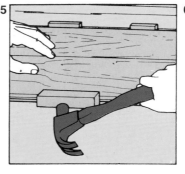

1 Spreading adhesive on a solid floor with a notched spreader. To fix the strips to a wood floor, nail through the lugs with panel pins.
2 Fitting the groove of the next strip over the lugs of the previous one; the strips may also be laid in herringbone pattern.
3 Floating wood strip flooring; metal clips fit between grooves under adjacent boards, joining them to each other but not to the floor beneath.

4 Applying woodworking adhesive to the groove of next board; maintain the expansion gap around the edges with wedges against the baseboard.
5 Tapping the groove onto the tongue of the previous board using a block of wood to protect the tongue; align end joints in alternate rows.
6 Covering the expansion gap with quadrant molding; pin the molding to the baseboard only, so that the boards may move beneath it.

wooden wedges of the correct thickness between the wall and the first board. Join strips by the method recommended by the manufacturer. Where lengths have to be cut to complete a strip, stagger the joins.

When the floor has been covered replace the baseboard or fit beading to conceal the expansion gap. Pre-finished floors will not need sealing, unsealed floors may need sanding and sealing (pages 42–44).

CHAPTER 5

TILES AND PANELING

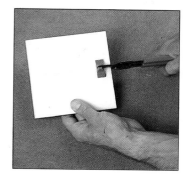

There are many advantages to covering walls and ceilings with ceramic tiles, particularly in shower units, toilets and utility rooms, for example, where they provide waterproof and easily-cleaned surfaces. The natural beauty of wood paneling, on the other hand, evokes warmth and a timeless quality that makes it ideal for interiors of any period style.

This chapter offers all the information you need for fixing tiles and paneling the professional way, with tips for cutting and shaping to give a perfect fit — thus making sure that you will be justly proud of the end results.

CERAMIC TILES

In certain areas of the house ceramic tiles may be preferred as a wallcovering, for example, around a shower, bath, basin or sink and will provide a waterproof background.

These tiles are available in a wide range of colors, patterns and prices.

Standard tiles come as either "field" or "edge" (border) tiles: the former are glazed only on their faces, their edges being concealed by the surrounding tiles; the latter have an exposed edge rounded and off and glazed. However these tiles are rapidly becoming obsolete, as manufacturers are turning to the "universal" tile, which has all four edges glazed: it can be used as a field or an edge tile.

Ceramic tiles are available in various sizes: from 2in sq to 12in sq. The most common sizes are 4in sq, 6in sq and $8 \frac{1}{2} \times 4 \frac{1}{4}$in rectangles. Tiles vary in thickness from $\frac{3}{16}$ to $\frac{1}{4}$in.

Some ceramic wall tiles have spacer lugs on the sides so that they can be set at an equal distance apart for grouting. If the tiles do not have lugs, plastic spacers can be bought to fit on the tiles. They sit flat on the wall and do not have to be removed prior to grouting. Alternatively you can use matchsticks.

Ceramic tiles should be applied with a waterproof adhesive specially formulated for ceramic wall tiles.

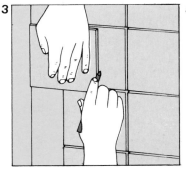
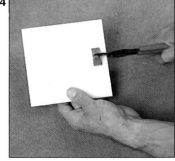

1 After determining the best starting point, fitting horizontal and vertical guide battens to the wall, crossing at this point.
2 Starting in the corner, laying the first tiles; press them firmly into the adhesive and insert spacers if the tiles are square-edge.

3 After removing battens, mark the width of an edge tile; hold it over the last full tile and mark along another against the side wall.
4 Cutting tiles by scoring a line along a straight-edge and breaking between the jaws of the tile cutter; also score rounded edges of tiles.

Surface preparation
As with any decoration, the surface behind tiles must be clean and sound. Strip off wallpaper and scrape away flaking paint. Wash well to remove dirt and allow to dry. Sand lightly to produce a key. If the plaster is powdery paint it with a stabilizing primer.

Sorting ceramic tiles
The colored glaze on tiles may differ slightly so it is advisable to check them. Also, separate those tile to be used for edging and corner edging. If plain and patterned tiles are to be mixed, arrange them on the floor to assess the effect of the design. It is much easier to do this in advance on the floor, rather than trying to visualize the effect on the wall.

Setting out ceramic wall tiles
This is the correct procedure for all ceramic and other small tiles, mirror or metal. The tiles are fixed to the wall, working upwards from the bottom, whether this be the baseboard, the edge of a shower tray, a bath, sink or basin. It is essential that the first row of tiles be absolutely straight and it is unlikely that any of these fixtures is that, so battens are used to set them squarely and support them while the adhesive sets.

First of all make a gauge from a long length of wood by striking off in tile width increments (plus any grouting gaps necessary). Use the gauge to plot how many whole tiles you will be able to fit in the wall height: aim for borders at top and bottom that are no less than half a tile wide. Mark the wall to indicate the perimeter of the field of whole tiles.

Plot the tile positions across the width of the wall, mark suitably wide borders. Next, temporarily nail a straight-edged length of $2 \times \frac{1}{2}$in softwood batten horizontally to the wall with its top edge level with field perimeter mark. Place a spirit level on the batten (into which you should first drive nails at 12in intervals so they just break through on the opposite side for easier fixing) to check the level. Tap in the nails so the batten is held against the wall. The first row of tiles is fitted along this batten, the tiles beneath being trimmed to fit the profile of the baseboard, or whatever you are tiling against.

Having set the horizontal support, the vertical

must be marked. A plumbline is used for this; drop a plumbline through this point and nail a batten to the outside of the line. It should be at an exact right angle to the horizontal batten. Check with some loose tiles.

Fixing ceramic wall tiles

Fix all the full tiles first, cutting in at the ends of walls and around features afterwards when the tiles are set firmly and the battens can be moved. With careful cutting one tile can be used to fill two gaps that are each less than a tile width in size.

Apply the recommended tiling adhesive to the wall with a notched applicator. Do not attempt to cover an area greater than one square yard at a time.

Press the tiles into the adhesive with a slight twisting movement to form suction with the ridges of adhesive. Work across the wall in horizontal rows, setting the tiles lug to lug if they have them, fitting spacers if they have not. Wipe off any adhesive that squeezes through the joins with a damp cloth.

When all the field tiles are stuck up, allow about 12 hours for the adhesive to set firm and then remove the battens. Cut and fit tiles to fill in the borders.

Tiling around fixtures

On reaching the basin, for instance, fix a batten above it, its top edge level with the line of full tiles to the side. Tile from this horizontal upwards. Cut in the tiles to fit around the basin later.

Cutting ceramic wall tiles

Ceramic wall tiles are not too difficult to break. Once the glazed surface is scored through with a tile cutter, the tile can be snapped along that line. The scoring must be done firmly to ensure a clean break.

To measure the tiles for filling a straight border, lay the tile over the tile nearest the edge, offer up a spare tile to overlap it and score down the line lightly. Score again firmly before breaking the tile over a matchstick. Smooth the rough cut edges with a carborundum stone or file.

Pincer-type tile cutters are a fairly cheap and accurate means of cutting tiles: they usually incorporate a wheel scoring disc and jaws into which the tile is placed, then snapped using scissor action.

As ceramic tiles have to be cut from the front, it is easier to mark the cut lines on the front, always using the spare tiles to indicate these lines. Shapes such as an L to fit around an obstruction should be scored and then bitten away little by little with a pair of pincers. A tile-cutting hacksaw blade is useful for curving cuts. A hole in the middle of the tile is cut by scoring a line

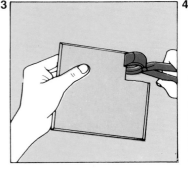

1 After spreading adhesive in the gap (or on the back of the tile if the gap is too narrow), pressing the cut tile into position.
2 Tiling an external corner; lay the edge of one tile flush with the side wall and overlap its edge with the tile covering the adjacent wall.

3 Cutting out a corner from a tile; after scoring the cutting line with a tile cutter, nibbling away the corner with pincers.
4 After allowing the recommended time for the adhesive to dry, filling the gaps between tiles with grout using a sponge.

through the center of the hole, breaking the tile along the line, then pincing out the two half circles.

On external corners, the tile on one wall is cut to fit the space exactly. The tile on the facing wall, which will be one of those with a glazed edge, is cut to overlap this raw edge, giving a neat finish.

In recesses that are greater than one tile in depth, the full tiles are placed around the front of the recess, butting over those on the surrounding wall, and cut tiles are positioned at the back. Where it is awkward to apply adhesive to the wall, use the back of the tile.

Grouting

Grouting is applied as a thick paste after all the tiles have been firmly adhered for several hours.

Spread it over the joins between the tiles with a flat spreader (usually one edge of the adhesive applicator is intended for this), wiping it off the tiles and into the joins. Wipe down with a damp sponge or cloth. When beginning to harden, pull the blunt end of a pencil along the lines of grout. When completely dry, wipe over with a clean dry cloth.

PANELING WALLS AND CEILINGS

Wood has a natural beauty and a certain charm that makes paneling feel right in any style of property.

Buying the paneling

Buy tongued-and-grooved matchboarding; knotty pine is the most popular, although you may prefer mahogany, cedar or ramin.

Standard T & G boards give a flush surface when the tongues are slotted into the grooves; tongued, grooved and V-jointed (TGV) types have a bevel cut on their top edges to create a fine V-shaped recess when the boards are connected, highlighting the paneled effect.

Matchboarding is sold in various lengths up to 10ft in nominal widths of 4in and a thickness of ½in. Actual sizes (due to planing) may be ⅜in less all round.

Wood paneling can also be bought in kit form from some lumber supply houses. The shrink-wrapped wood comes in 8ft or 9ft lengths, 4in wide and ½in or ⅝in thick. Packs commonly contain 16 lengths. Some come with special clips for fixing. The various moldings needed for finishing off at corners, ceilings and baseboards can be bought in separate packs.

When buying, examine the boards for warps, splits and loose knots. Take the room measurements to the lumber yard to confirm the number of boards required: basically the width (or height) of the wall divided by the width of the board, taking into account the length of the boards required and allowing for joins. Buy a few extra to allow for wastage.

Methods of fixing

The paneling is either pinned to battens or, on a hollow partition wall, can be pinned direct to the vertical studs and horizontal bracing; find the position of the framing by tapping the wall and mark them as a guide for the pinning of the paneling.

When battens are being used added insulation can be incorporated by fitting polystyrene sheet or mineral fiber blanket between the battens. To protect against condensation it is advisable to hang a sheet of plastic flat to the wall behind the battens.

The battens should be 1 × 2in sawn wood. They should be fixed at 2ft intervals, running in the opposite direction to the paneling and must be absolutely horizontal (or vertical). The arrangement of the battens will be affected by the way the paneling is to be arranged (see diagram). They must be nailed or screwed to the wall at the point where joins in the paneling are to be made, in order to support them.

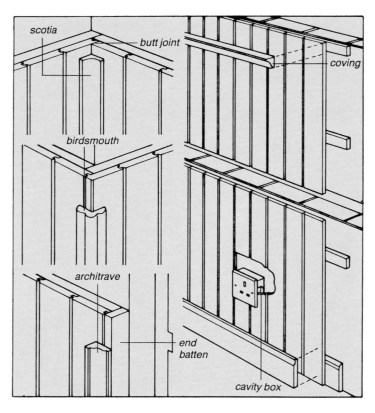

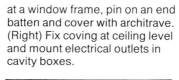

(Left) Finish off an internal corner with scotia molding pinned over the butt-joined boards, and use birdsmouth molding at an external corner; at a window frame, pin on an end batten and cover with architrave. (Right) Fix coving at ceiling level and mount electrical outlets in cavity boxes.

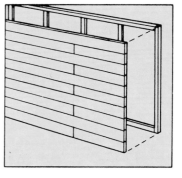

An outer frame and intermediate vertical battens support horizontal paneling; butt join the ends of boards over a batten.

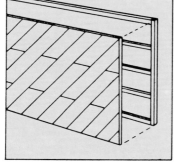

For diagonal panelling the battens run horizontally; stagger the ends in adjacent rows and align them in alternate rows.

The paneling is secret-nailed through the tongue at an angle into the batten so as not to be visible on the surface; the groove of the adjoining board conceals the fixing. Electrical fixtures may need to be re-mounted flush with the paneling.

Fixing the battens

Fix the battens vertically or horizontally, according to the choice of paneling, with 2 ½in masonry nails or 2

½in No. 8 countersunk woodscrews. Drive in the nails so that they just break through the wood before positioning the batten against the wall. Check that it is level (use a spirit level) and drive the nails fully home. With screws, pre-drill pilot holes in the batten, mark the wall, drill for plugs and then screw into position.

Not only must the battens be level but also their faces must lie flat. Check this with a straight-edged plank of wood and pack out any irregularities with offcuts of hardboard. An existing baseboard can act as a horizontal batten and may also need padding out.

At an external corner, butt the end of one batten to the face of another. Fit extra battens around windows and doors.

Fixing the paneling

Cut the first board to length and offer it up to the wall, tongue outwards. Check that it is straight with a spirit level or plumbline. If not, it can either be scribed to fit or a slight gap left which can later be concealed with a length of molding.

To scribe the board, fix it temporarily to the wall, absolutely straight. Place a small block of wood on the board, one edge pressed to the side wall, and hold a pencil against the outer edge: tape the pencil to the block. Run the two down the board to mark the wall profile and saw along the pencil line with a rip saw.

Fix the first board in position tongue outermost and secure it firmly to the battens with 1in long panel pins knocked through the tongue at an angle of 45 degrees. (On wood-framed walls, use 1¼in long nails). Offer up the next board, slot the groove over the tongue. Tap it in close, at the top, middle and bottom, protecting the edge of the board with an offcut. Continue fixing the paneling across the wall.

At an external corner, plane off the tongue and/or cut the board down to overlap the corner by the thickness of the paneling. Butt the grooved edge of the board on the other side of the angle up to it. Conceal the joint with right-angled molding.

Fit the paneling close to doors and windows and nail on new architrave to conceal the edges.

To avoid difficulty in fitting the last board into an internal angle, do not secure the previous two boards, but instead slot the three together, position the groove of the first one over the tongue of the last board on the wall and snap the three into place for a tight fit. Butt the first board on the facing wall into the corner and conceal the join with molding.

Fit ceiling molding and new baseboard to conceal the cut edges at the top and bottom of the wall.

For ceilings the principle is the same as that for

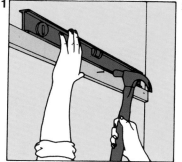

1 After hammering masonry nails into the batten, nailing it horizontally to the wall over a vapor barrier of plastic sheeting.
2 Before hammering the nails fully home, inserting shims of wood to pack out low areas; check for level.
3 Fitting cut slabs of styrofoam between the battens to provide insulation; no fixing is needed.
4 Holding the first board vertically, groove against an uneven end wall, and scribing onto the board; cut and pin in place, tongue outwards.
5 Knocking the groove of the second board over the tongue of the first by hammering against an offcut; check that the board is vertical.
6 Pinning the board to the battens by hammering 1in long panel pins through the tongue at 45° and punching below the surface.

walls, with battens being fixed at intervals across the ceiling. A special ceiling molding can be fitted all the way around to conceal both cut ends of boards.

Sealing the paneling

The wood must be sealed or it will quickly become dirty. Varnish gives it a tough finish, and you can also apply stain or wood dye.

CHAPTER 6
PAINTING OUTSIDE

While any exterior painting of a house should be considered as a decorative feature, it is primarily meant to preserve and protect the surface from the elements. Wood is especially prone to the effects of moisture and should be repainted on a regular basis for best results.

Details of how to do this, along with painting walls and exterior metalwork, are shown in this chapter. Information is also given for choosing the appropriate equipment and the techniques used in painting the highest points of the house. Armed with this professional advice, the home improver is assured of excellent results that will greatly improve a property for many years to come.

PAINTING EXTERIOR WALLS

Although painting the exterior walls of your house is primarily meant to revive its appearance, the treatment is equally important to protect the structure from the effects of the weather; paint deteriorates more rapidly outside a house than inside because of the harsh treatment it receives. Not only does it have to contend with severe variations in temperature but also a regular dashing with rain and wind, which, at best, will leave it looking dirty – at worst, will cause problems with damp, rot and a general breakdown in the structure.

The most important thing to remember when contemplating painting walls that have previously been left plain is that, once painted, the finish will have to be maintained on a regular basis.

The answer for brick walls that look good as they are is to paint them with a clear water repellant. This prevents the penetration of moisture, while at the same time, preserving the condition of the brickwork without altering its natural appearance.

Planning to paint
It is not necessary to paint the entire house at one time. Adopt a regular cycle, by treating one or two elevations a year, then dealing with the others the next, then repeating the process every four or five years. The weather should be warm but the sun not too hot: a calm, dry day between late spring and early autumn is ideal.

When repainting, it is quite likely that one wall will be in far worse condition than the others, because it is in a more exposed position. This wall may need repainting on a more regular basis than the rest of the house. However, do not create work for yourself: do not paint sheltered walls that are in good condition, unless of course a change in color is planned.

It is sensible to carry out a regular check on the condition of the exterior paintwork; here is some guidance as to the regularity with which certain checks should be carried out. A house in a city or town is likely to need more regular treatment than one in the country.

For all houses, clear the gutters of debris each year and check the condition of downpipes. Check over and clean ledges and sills every two years. Nothing will ruin the paintwork more rapidly than leaking gutters, downpipes and window sills with clogged drip grooves, which allow water to trickle onto the wall surface instead of throwing it clear.

On a city house a paint finish should last for at least five years, if it has been properly applied; in country areas it could last twice as long.

Never leave paintwork until the paint reaches the point of cracking and lifting – rainwater will seep underneath and adversely affect the wood. If it is caught before this stage the preparation will be much easier and quicker to carry out.

Industrial pollution is a major hazard in towns and cities and, although the paintwork may be in good repair, it will be dirty: a rigid policy of washing down annually will keep it looking in trim.

Preparing to paint
Adequate preparation of exterior paintwork is vital, even though the finished appearance may not be as important as interior finishes: the protective qualities are paramount. Full details on preparing exterior walls and some common repairs that may be necessary are given on pages 9–15.

Carry out all preparation first, of walls, woodwork and metal, so that there is no danger of paint chippings or cleaning agents falling on newly painted surfaces. Work from the top of the house down for the same reason.

Types of exterior wall finishes

Brick New brickwork must be allowed to dry out for at least three months before any painting is attempted.

If in any doubt of the stability of old brickwork, painted or plain, paint it first liberally with a stabilizing solution; this will give a sound base on which to decorate. One coat of primer is sufficient. If you are going to use resin-based paint, apply an all-surface primer instead.

Stucco Always looks better painted. If the finish is fairly smooth it will be possible to use a roller. Rough cast rendering, which tends to hold more dirt than smooth surfaces, will need a particularly thorough cleaning before being painted with a large whitewash brush.

Rough stucco This tends to deteriorate more rapidly than other wall finishes because any movement in the mortar, shrinking or expansion, causes cracks which lift the pebbles and will eventually fall off leaving bald patches. Paint will conceal many of the defects very effectively, sealing small cracks and preventing further deterioration. It makes repairs simpler, as the color of the pebbles used to fill bald patches will not matter if they are to be painted over. To ensure good paint coverage, particularly to the mortar between the pebbles, it is best to use a lambswool roller or large whitewhash brush.

Stone The easiest surface to paint, being the smoothest. Use a roller for speed. If the surface is powdery or stained, use a stabilizing solution as a primer.

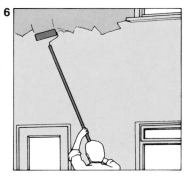

1 Painting a rough stucco wall using a dustpan brush, after masking downpipes with newspaper, to ensure that the mortar is also painted.
2 After filling a wide bucket ⅓ full with paint, pulling the loaded roller over a board to ensure uniform coverage.
3 Starting at the top right-hand corner (if right-handed), cutting in under the eaves with a brush, taking care not to overstretch.
4 Again working from the right if right-handed, painting a row of vertical, slightly overlapping strips with the roller.
5 After completing one width of the wall, painting a second series of strips, working in easy-to-reach stages across the wall.
6 Near ground level, using the roller with an extension handle to avoid having to dismount and remount the ladder for each strip.

Aids to painting

The main problem is access to the upper areas of the house. An option to a ladder is scaffolding, which you can rent: towers of different heights, ending in a wooden platform and ones fitted with castors for mobility (without having to dismantle the sections) are a good choice. When erecting the tower; beware of positioning it too close to the wall, making it difficult to reach the area immediately in front of the scaffolding. Do not forget to lock any castors before you mount the tower. When using a ladder, choose an extension type fitted with a ladder stay, which clips over the top rung of the ladder and supports it away from the wall and guttering: the stay is wider than the ladder and has a much better grip, so it is not likely to slip sideways. It also makes it much easier to attach a paint kettle to an upper rung; this can hang in front of the painter, making it easy to reload a brush or roller while keeping one hand on the ladder all the time for personal safety.

The painting of large areas is greatly speeded by using a roller and many rollers can be fitted with an extension pole, allowing the painter to work without a ladder in lower areas and extending the reach of a ladder in upper areas. And speedier still for painting large areas, is the spray gun (see page 67).

Painting the walls

Follow the sun around the house starting on the wall it has just left, so that it has time to dry out the surface before you reach it. The positioning of the ladder is important. For right-handed people, erect it at the right-side of the wall, about 24in from the end. Paint the wall to the right only; do not try to paint from both sides of the ladder. When this area is finished, move the ladder to the left and paint the next area. This way, the ladder is always being moved onto unpainted areas. If you are left-handed, reverse the process.

Always start at the top of the wall. Aim always to have a wet edge of paint to brush into the next area being painted; dried edges will show and exterior wall paint dries very quickly.

Paint the whole wall in one go or stop only at an obvious break-off point: where a downpipe divides a wall, it is acceptable to paint the two halves separately, so long as the same paint mix is used. The joining line will be concealed by the pipe. Likewise, paint definite "bays" formed by corners of walls, windows and door frames.

Always apply the paint generously and wash off splashes promptly as the paint dries quickly.

Paint for exterior walls

The various special paints suitable for all types of masonry are listed below.

● Exterior grade latex is similar to the indoor type; a water-based liquid that dries to a smooth, matt finish. More durable than its indoor counterpart, it comes in a wide range of colors and contains a mold-resisting

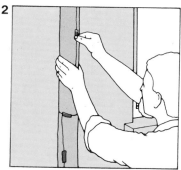

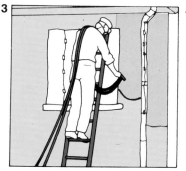

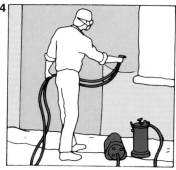

1 Masking off windows with large sheets of paper or plastic before painting walls with a spray-gun; lay dust-sheets on the ground.
2 Mask drainpipes with newspaper. Work from the bottom upwards; stick joints between sheets, and edges with masking tape.
3 After thinning the paint as recommended for the equipment, spraying towards breaks in the wall, such as downpipes.

4 Continue downwards in horizontal strips; spray over edges of all masked-off areas and keep the gun at right-angles to the wall.
5 Removing the masking tape from masked-off areas before the paint has dried, otherwise the paint may peel away with it.
6 Painting the remaining areas with a brush; use a small brush to cut in round door and window frames and to paint behind downpipes.

additive. It is usual to apply a thinned priming coat on porous walls, followed by one or two full strength coats for a good finish.
● Reinforced latex is a water-thinnable, spirit-based liquid with added fine aggregate (such as mica) for a finely textured finish. Two coats are necessary and the paint will cover hairline cracks.

● Cement paint is the cheapest exterior wall paint and comes as a dry powder which you mix with water in the proportions 2:1. There is a limited range of colors, but clean sand can be added to give extra protection on an exposed wall.
● Stone paint is a durable treatment for any type of masonry, capable of filling minor cracks in walls.
● Masonry paint is a resin-based paint which dries to a tough, semi-gloss finish. It should be applied in a thinned first coat (using white spirit) to prime the surface for a further two full-strength coats.

PAINTING EXTERIOR JOINERY

Exterior woodwork suffers deterioration much more rapidly than any other part of the house. This is basically because wood is extremely sensitive to moisture. Rising moisture content in the wood is stronger than the paint film covering it and will break through, lifting the paint with disastrous results.

Obviously, exterior woodwork is also subject to constant attack by moisture, from rain, early morning dew and, possibly, at lower levels, from dampness in the soil.

Preparing to paint
Details of preparing wood for painting are given on page 12–13.

Remember always to prime bare patches and prime areas that are to be filled both before and after filling. Make sure the primer is absorbed well into the wood.

Never paint in full sun: the heat will accelerate the drying process unnaturally and the paint may wrinkle, flake off or blister. Do not be tempted to start painting too early in the morning either, as dew could easily ruin a smooth coat of paint, thinning and streaking it.

Painting soffits, bargeboards and fascias
Being situated at the top of the house, these are the areas of wood to paint first. According to the choice of paint, apply one coat of undercoat after the wood has been sanded down, filled and spot-primed. Although primer can be left uncovered for a few days, undercoat cannot. The first application of top coat should follow within 48 hours.

The finish of the top coat is unimportant from an appearance point of view as these areas are well above eye level. Make sure a good covering of paint is applied, though, for protection purposes. Being high up and, therefore more exposed, these areas are particularly vulnerable to the elements. Although two

1 Painting a soffit with a brush; spot-prime any chips, undercoat and apply at least two liberal coats of enamel paint.
2 Protecting shiplap wood cladding with an oil-based exterior varnish; do not use polyurethane varnish as it breaks down in sunlight.
3 Spot-priming chipped paintwork; when the primer has dried, fill the chip level with the surface, smooth, reprime and paint.

painting the inside (see page 21), according to the type of door being painted. The highest level of finish is needed, particularly on the front door, and the work should not be hurried.

Remember also to paint both the top and bottom edges of the door, to prevent water penetration.

Painting windows
Paint the upper windows first, following the same sequence as for painting the inside (see page 22). Use a paint guard or masking tape to protect the edge of the glass. When painting over the putty, extend the paint on to the glass by about $\frac{1}{8}$in to provide a waterproof seal against damp, protecting both the putty and wood frame.

Windowsills: wooden sills have a drip groove on their underside, running the length of the sill, designed to prevent rainwater dripping over the edge of the sill and running back along the underside into the wall. Keep this clear of debris and excess paint. The underside should be painted for protection.

coats of enamel should be sufficient, an extra one could be worthwhile. Apply the paint more generously than on interior surfaces.

Painting cladding
The largest area of wood likely to be found on a house is wood cladding. It is essential that the edges and end grain are thoroughly protected to prevent moisture penetration.

A large brush can be used to speed the operation slightly. Do not bother rubbing down between coats. If the paint is applied as directed on the can, observing the drying times, this will be unnecessary.

Painting exterior doors
The exterior doors should always be the last area of wood to be painted on the house.

Follow the sequence for painting that is given for

Rubbing down a steel window frame with steel wool to remove rust and to provide a key on the painted areas for the new paint.

After wiping off all traces of rust and debris with a clean cloth, applying a coat of primer over the bare metal areas.

PAINTING EXTERIOR METALWORK

The painting of exterior metalwork is often the final bit of decorating to be done. For those with no metalwork on the house itself it can be tempting to

Paints for exterior woodwork

It is advisable to buy one of the brands of paint specially formulated for exterior wood. These allow the wood to "breathe" allowing moisture to escape in the form of water vapour.

Several brands are available, some having the added advantage that they need no primer or undercoat. The paint is applied direct to the prepared wood

and dries to a smooth sheen rather than a high gloss. Specially formulated gloss paint is also available but this does require the usual primer and undercoat.

An alternative to paint is varnish – ideal where you want to retain the natural graining of the wood. Again there are specially-formulated brands for exterior use such as yacht varnish.

Another finish that maintains the natural appearance of the wood is a decorative wood preservative combining a water repellent with a wood preserver and a color pigment. This will restore the color to wood that has been bleached by the weather and has become gray, while protecting it from further attack by both moisture and insects.

put the brushes away after the final touch has been given to the doors. But even a single gate needs the protection that sound paintwork provides and there is little point in having a property to be proud of when the entrance is an eye-sore.

It is only too obvious when metal is deteriorating, rust being the noticeable effect. Although extensive corrosion can look alarming, with today's special treatments even the worst areas can be dealt with.

Preparing to paint

This has been made much easier with the rust-neutralizer treatments that are now available. However, these are not always necessary and, where the rust is not extensive and is easily brushed away, a rust-inhibiting primer will be sufficient. Do apply this liberally; it is the most important stage in the decorating procedure.

Paints for exterior metalwork

Gloss enamel paint is that most commonly used. There are now enamel paints that are particularly formulated for metal, although they can be used on woodwork too.

These paints are very tough and will transform a pitted surface into one that is smooth and glossy: one brand gives a beaten metal effect, particularly attractive on railings and gates. The surface must be sanded to provide a key and all loose rust removed, but it is not essential to remove all the old paintwork and firm dry rust. Old paint should be cleaned thoroughly to remove all traces of grease and dirt.

Most ordinary paints are applied with a brush, spray or roller. Only one generous coat is needed but it may be easier with vertical surfaces to apply two thinner coats and thus avoid sags and runs in the paint. The paint is touch-dry in 30 minutes so the waiting between coats is minimal.

The thicker the finish the better. It should be the equivalent of four coats of ordinary gloss paint.

Painting metal doors and windows

These require the same careful protection as wooden doors and windows and should be painted in the same sequence as the insides. Be careful to protect the top and bottom edges with a good coating of primer and paint. Although the paint coat needs to be thick, several thin coats applied one on top of the other will be more satisfactory and the problem of sags and runs will be avoided. On windows and glazed doors, remember to continue the paint over the putty to form a watertight seal on the glass.

Painting gutters

Cast iron gutters needs regular maintenance. The best treatment for new or repaired lengths of gutters is to paint the inside with a bituminous paint. This resists the corrosive effects of rain and there is no need to prime the metal first.

For the decoration of the outside of the gutters and the downpipes, having primed the metal with a zinc chromate primer, apply one undercoat and two top coats of enamel. Protect the wall behind the downpipes with a piece of card. Splashes of enamel paint on the wall are difficult to remove and look unsightly. A small paint pad on a long handle can be useful for getting round the back of pipes that are set close to the wall.

When the condition of the gutters is such that replacement is a consideration, the type requiring least maintenance is plastic. It comes in either white or gray and needs no paint protection. Should the color be changed though, clean the plastic with white spirit or turpentine and apply two coats of enamel paint. There is no need to prime or undercoat plastic.

1 Brushing off rust from a cast iron soil or rainwater downpipe using a wire brush; check that all fixings are securely in the wall.
2 Protecting the wall behind a downpipe with masonite to prevent paint splashes; pay particular attention to the back of the pipe.
3 Drying guttering with a cloth after removing all rust and debris and washing out thoroughly with a hosepipe or plenty of water.
4 Painting the inside of cast iron guttering with black bitumen paint after sealing any leaking joints with bitumen cement.

Picture credit:
P.33, Wall coverings by Dorma, PO Box 7, Lees Street, Swinton, Manchester M27 2DD, England.